Free Stuff

FOR

Doll Lovers

ON THE

INTERNET

Judy Heim and Gloria Hansen

C&T PUBLISHING

Copyright © 2000 Judy Heim and Gloria Hansen
Developmental Editor: Barbara Kuhn
Technical Editor: Steve Cook
Cover and Book Design: Christina Jarumay
Illustration: Christina Jarumay and Claudia Böhm
Book Production: Claudia Böhm
Production Co-ordinator: Diane Pedersen
Production Assistants: Stacy Chamness and Kirstie L. McCormick

We take great care to ensure that the information included in this book is
accurate and presented in good faith, but no warranty is provided nor results
guaranteed. Since we have no control over the choice of materials or procedure used, neither the authors nor C&T Publishing, Inc. shall have any liability
to any person or entity with respect to any loss or damage caused directly or
indirectly by the information contained in this book.

Library of Congress Cataloging-in-Publication Data

Heim, Judy.
      Free stuff for doll lovers on the Internet /
Judy Heim and Gloria Hansen.
      p.   cm.
      Includes index.
      ISBN 1-57120-108-4 (paper trade)
      1. Dollmaking--Computer network resources--Directories.
2. Dolls--Collectors and collecting--Computer network resources--Directories.
3. Internet addresses--Directories. 4. Web sites--Directories. 5. Free material--
Computer network resources--Directories. I. Hansen, Gloria. II. Title.
      TT175.H39 2000
      025.06'6887221--dc21
                        00-009820
                        CIP

Published by C&T Publishing
P.O. Box 1456
Lafayette, California 94549

Printed in China
10 9 8 7 6 5 4 3 2 1

DEDICATION

We dedicate this book to Barb Kuhn, editorial earth mother, patroness of sanity, Silicon Valley turbo-mom, our link to all that is new and exciting in the Army Reserve, and the living doll in our lives. Without her this series of books would not have been possible—nor would it have been very good. Thanks, Barb!

There are thousands of Web sites for doll lovers. Sifting through them was a challenge. While we've tried to select sites that we think offer the most doll making and collecting advice, that doesn't mean there aren't many more out there that are equally illuminating and valuable. Also, because of the fluid nature of the Internet, it is inevitable that some of the Web sites in this book may have moved or even vanished. Had we included only those Web sites that are sure to be around many moons from now, this book wouldn't be nearly as valuable.

Symbols in this book

 You can find lots of free goodies on the Web, but you'll learn more if you follow the chat icons to the many discussion groups offered on the Internet.

 This icon signifies a bit of Judy and Gloria's hard-earned wisdom--in other words, something we wished we knew when we first started cruising the Web.

 When you see this icon, read carefully—and don't make one of the same silly mistakes we have!

 This icon tells you that the Web site sells merchandise related to the free information that they offer.

Table of Contents

1 Join The Doll Fun on the Web 6

- This Book Will Show You the Way to Doll Fun
  on the Web Faster than Anything Else Will............................ 6
- America Online Is a Good Place to Get Started
  If You've Never Been Online Before 7
- Tips for Tapping Into Doll Making and
  Collecting Advice on America Online 8
- How to Tap into Doll-Making Web Sites Through AOL 12
- More Tips for Viewing Doll Web Sites with AOL 12
- If You Outgrow AOL and Decide to Shop
  for an Internet Service... 14
- What Doll Lovers Need to Know About Their Web Browser.. 16
- How to Tap Into a Web Page.. 18
- Find Your Way Around the Web Without Getting Lost 23
- How to Use Bookmarks... 24
- Printing Web Pages and Saving Pictures to Disk 29
- Judy & Gloria's Ten-Step Program
  for Fixing Browser and Graphics Crashes 30
- How to Send E-Mail 34
- How to Read Usenet Newsgroups with Your Web Browser.... 35
- Tips for Staying Safe on the Web....................................... 40

2 free Big Web Sites for Doll Makers 42

3 free Big Web Sites for Doll Collectors 45

- More Web Sites for Doll Collectors 48
- Web Sites for Collectors of Specific Sorts of Dolls................. 50
- Bulletin Boards for Doll Collectors 54
- Surf Web Rings to Visit the Web Sites
  of Other Doll Collectors 55

4 free Doll-Making Hangouts in Cyberspace 56

5 free Help for Making Cloth Dolls 66

6 free Cloth Doll and Doll Clothing Patterns 71

7 free Help for Making Porcelain and Clay Dolls 80

8 free Help Caring for and Restoring Dolls 89

9 free Big Web Sites for Teddy Bear Makers 97

10 free Discussions for Teddy Bear Makers and Lovers..106

11 free Teddy Bear Patterns...108

12 free Teddy Bear-Making Tips and How-Tos..................111

13 free Help Finding Doll and Bear-Making Supplies 114

- Web Auction Sites Are Dynamite Places to
  Shop for Doll Stuff..664

- More of Judy & Gloria's Tips for Shopping for
  Doll Stuff on the Web 115

- Directories of Retailers of
  Hard-to-Find Doll-Making Supplies........................117

- Surf the Web Sites of Doll Artists for Great Patterns..121

- More Web Auction Sites for Doll Lovers........................... 123

- How to Find An Out of Print or Otherwise Hard to Find
  Doll Pattern or Book on the Web..................................... 130

- Judy & Gloria's Tips for Fabric Shopping on the Web.......... 131

14 free Web Sites of Doll Magazines, Clubs, and Museums .. 133

15 free Patterns and Advice for Making

Dolls and Bears for Charity... 146

16 free Patterns for Knitting and Crocheting Dolls,

Teddies, and Their Clothes   152

17 free Help for Doll Houses... 157

18 free Help for Sewing, Smocking, and Embellishing Doll

Clothes.. 165

Index 172

About The Authors 173

Free Stuff on the Internet Series from C&T Publishing....174

CHAPTER 1
Join the Doll Fun
on the Web

Doll-makers and lovers are special people. They believe in the magic of a penciled face, curly wool for hair, and muslin for hands. They have no compunctions about decorating their living room with floppy beings that others might dismiss as toys. If you make or collect dolls, you'll find kindred spirits on the Web. You'll meet fun-loving doll makers eager to share wisdom. You'll meet other doll collectors who host Web sites that are chock-full of advice. There are also thousands of places to shop for hard-to-find doll-making supplies and tools, as well as for antique dolls and doll patterns. You'll be amazed at how the doll makers and resources available to you on the Web will catapult your doll making or collecting to new heights.

✪ THIS BOOK WILL SHOW YOU THE WAY TO DOLL FUN ON THE WEB FASTER THAN ANYTHING ELSE WILL

A few years ago you could tap just about any question into a Web search engine like Altavista **(http://www.altavista.com)** and find an answer with just a few mouse clicks. These days it's not so easy. The Web has exploded into the world's biggest library and shopping mall, with millions of Web sites and tens of thousands of discussion groups. Sorting through them to find what you need can be an arduous task. We've done the work for you. We've sifted through thousands of doll collecting and making Web sites and organized the best into chapters that will speed you to:

- Free patterns—for doll bodies, as well as doll and teddy clothes.
- Free how-tos for fashioning doll bodies, sculpting faces, styling hair, and more.
- Web sites with doll and teddy repair help.
- Web sites with valuable information for collectors, such as how to store and display your doll.
- Advice on restoring and preserving antique dolls.
- Web sites with advice on where to shop for hard-to-find doll supplies.

AMERICA ONLINE IS A GOOD PLACE TO GET STARTED IF YOU'VE NEVER BEEN ONLINE BEFORE

AOL is a great way to get started on the Internet if you've never tapped into cyberspace before. But be warned, you may outgrow it fast. (Less than a month after after Judy and her husband got their parents on America Online, they were clamoring for faster access to the Web.)

You can get a free AOL startup disk by calling 800/827-6364, or have a friend download the software for you from **America Online**'s Web site **(http://www.aol.com)**.

Once you've installed the software and have connected to America Online, press **Ctrl-K** (or ⌘-**K** on a Mac) and type the keyword **INTERNET<ENTER>** or **WEB<ENTER>**. You're now on the Internet.

Among AOL's disadvantages are its hourly fees to access some areas of the service and the fact that the service's access numbers are long-distance calls for some. Also, AOL's numbers are sometimes busy in the evening (when all the kids are online). AOL also charges additional hourly access fees for anyone connecting from outside the continental United States or calling through an AOL 800 number.

TIPS FOR TAPPING INTO DOLL MAKING AND COLLECTING ADVICE ON AMERICA ONLINE

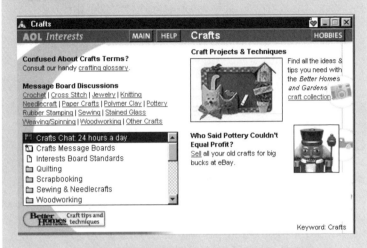

Use the keyword **crafts** to get to the main crafts area on America Online. You'll find message boards and file libraries for different craft categories.

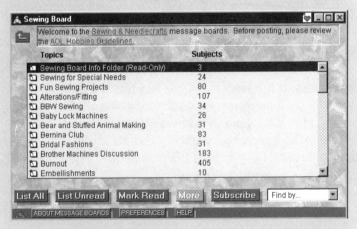

To chat with other doll makers, head to the sewing message board. Use the keyword **sewing**.

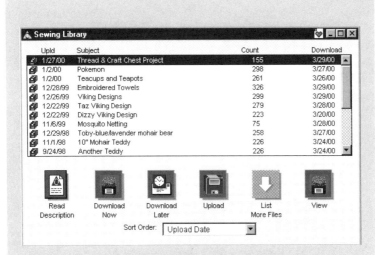

In the Sewing Library you'll find occasional free patterns for teddies and dolls, as well as doll-making advice.

Head to the main Crafts Community menu for a longer list of craft libraries and message boards.

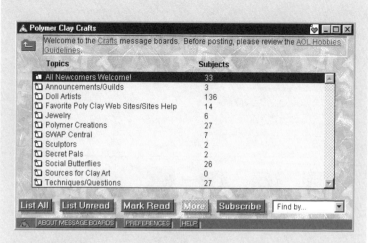

You'll find an active group of doll artists hanging out in the Polymer Crafting area on America Online. To get there, use the keyword **crafts** and select "polymer clay" under Message Board Discussions. There's also a polymer crafts library where you can download directions and advice.

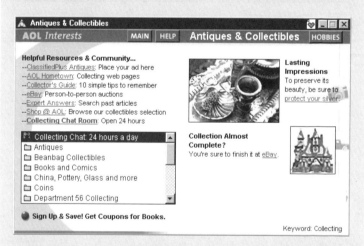

To get to the antique and collectibles area on America Online, use the keyword **collectibles**. Doll collectors were in short supply in these forums the last time we looked, but you'll find advice on preserving old, fragile things, such as antique dolls.

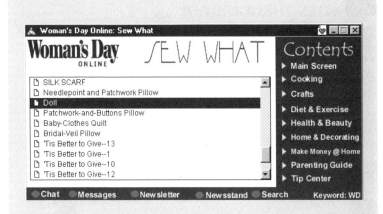

You'll also find doll makers chatting it up in the Woman's Day area on America Online. Use the keywords **womans day** *and select "crafts" from the menu. In the Crafts screen, use the scroll bars to head to the sewing and crafts message boards and libraries.*

HOW TO TAP INTO DOLL-MAKING WEB SITES THROUGH AOL

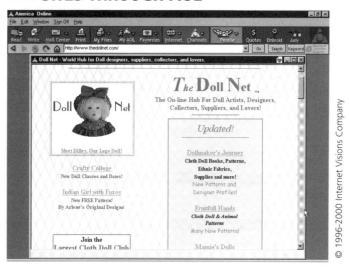

In order to visit a Web site while you're connected to AOL, type the Web site's URL (Uniform Resource Locator—a Web site's address, such as **http://www.ctpub.com**) into the keyword bar at the top of the screen. For example, when you type the URL for the popular Web site Doll Net (**http://www.thedollnet.com**), AOL will pop up this Web viewer window and take you to the Web site. But sometimes AOL can be confusing. **It can be hard to tell when you're on AOL and when you're on the Web**. If you type a word like "doll" into that keyword box—an obvious thing to do, which you might think would take you someplace—AOL's own toy-shopping Web site will pop up. Remember: if you see a URL appear in that keyword box, AOL has taken you out onto the Web.

More Tips for Viewing Doll Web Sites with AOL

Doll Web sites are full of pictures, but sometimes the pictures may look smeary or may not appear at all. Here are tips for troubleshooting picture problems:

Clear Up Smeary Pictures—If you use Internet Explorer 5 to surf the Web with AOL, you may have noticed that IE 5 sometimes has problems displaying Web graphics. The culprit is

AOL's graphics compression. Turn it off by heading to **My AOL/Preferences** and clicking the **WWW** icon. Head to the **Web Graphics** tab and remove the check beside "Use compressed graphics." Click **Apply**.

Clean Out Your Cache—Clean out AOL's cache directories and files regularly to keep the software from slowing down on the Web. Click **My AOL**, select **Preferences**, and click **WWW**. Under the **General** tab, click **Delete Files** under **Temporary Internet Files**, and, in the **History** category, click the **Clear History** button. While you're there, click the **Settings** button under **Temporary Internet Files** and reduce the "amount of disk space to use" to store Web graphics to about 50 megabytes. A large cache file can slow down your Web sessions. Run Scandisk weekly.

Try a Different Browser—If you'd rather surf the Web with Microsoft's Internet Explorer or Netscape, once you connect to AOL, minimize the AOL software and fire up your favorite browser instead.

Power Down to AOL 3.0—If AOL's software seems to run slowly on your PC and if you have an older computer—a 486, an older Pentium, or a Macintosh running System 7.5 or below—try installing an older version of AOL's software. You can download AOL 3.0 from AOL's Web site (**http://www.aol.com**).

Having Problems with Your America Online Connection? Head to the Members Helping Members forum on America Online for the best tech support on the service. Type the keywords **members helping members** in the location bar at the top of the screen to get there. This will take you to a public discussion area where you're sure to find other members who are having the same problem as you are—or who know the solution.

![bear] IF YOU OUTGROW AOL AND DECIDE TO SHOP FOR AN INTERNET SERVICE...

Many people graduate from AOL to an Internet service provider (ISP) with local access numbers because of the better speed and reliability an ISP gives them. Whether you sign up with a national ISP or a local one, shop for one with a fast connection (T1 or better, directly into the Internet's network backbone) and 56K bps connections that support the same connection standards as your modem. Ask friends and neighbors for recommendations (you don't want an ISP that inflicts busy signals or is slow at delivering e-mail). Most ISPs offer unlimited Internet access for $20/month. That usually includes the ability to set up a Web site. Five megs of Web space is a good size to get started with.

Our picks for favorite national ISPs?
AT&T's WorldNet (**http://www.att.net**) and Earthlink (**http://www.earthlink.com**).

Cable TV Offers High Speed Internet, but at a Price

Many local cable TV franchises offer Internet access through the same cable that sends you cable TV. With advertised connect rates of 10 megabytes per second, it's no wonder cable Internet is getting popular—although actual connect rates can be considerably lower, depending upon what time of day you tap in. Cable Internet costs about $150 for installation, plus $40 to $50 per month. (That may be a good deal if you're getting gouged by local phone rates to call AOL or an ISP.) Cable Internet is presently available in limited areas of the country, though access is sure to grow. To find out if you can get it, call your local cable TV franchise.

When you call for prices, ask how many outlets are included in the installation fee (cable TVs and cable modems can't connect to the same outlet), and make sure you can actually connect to the Internet before your cable installer leaves. You'll also need to find out if you get any space for a Web site; many cable companies don't offer the ability to set up a Web site.

Some people use a combination of America Online and cable access. If you decide to go this route, sign up for AOL's "Bring Your Own Access" subscription option for the cheapest rate.

Satellite Is Pricey,
but the Only Option in Some Rural Areas

If phone calls to the nearest ISP are eating into your lifestyle and cable Internet isn't available in your area, consider accessing the Internet via satellite. The main requirements are a Windows 95 or NT-running PC, a direct line of sight to the southern horizon, and a lot of patience. Hughes Network System's DirecPC (**http://www.direcpc.com**) is the leading satellite Internet service.

WHAT ABOUT "FREE E-MAIL" SERVICES?

There are two sorts of free e-mail services. There is **Juno** (**http://www.juno.com**) which gives you free software that you use to dial local access numbers and send and retrieve mail. And, there are Web-based services such as Microsoft's **Hotmail** (**http://www.hotmail.com**). You tap into these Web services through a computer that already has some Internet access—a work computer, for instance, or one at a library or cyber-cafe. Their advantage is that you can send and retrieve private e-mail through the service without using your work e-mail address when you tap in through your work computer, for example.

Juno is a great deal, especially if there's a local access number in your area. But all you get is e-mail, unless you pony up $20/month for Web access.

> ✋ ***Warning!*** There are some big disadvantages to using the "free e-mail" services like Juno and Hotmail. You may not be able to participate in some of the high-volume discussion mailing lists. These lists generate lots of e-mail each day—so much mail that it will quickly fill up your mail box on these services, causing the mailing list owner to unsubscribe you in irritation. In fact, some mailing lists won't even permit people to subscribe who are using free e-mail services like Hotmail or Yahoo. It's best to get a "real" e-mail account with an ISP or online service like America Online.

![bear] WHAT DOLL LOVERS NEED TO KNOW ABOUT THEIR WEB BROWSER

Whether you tap into the Web through an Internet service or America Online, the software centerpiece of your Web surfing is what's called a browser. In the old days you needed different sorts of software to do different things on the Net. For instance, you needed mail software to send and receive e-mail, a newsreader to read public discussions, and special software called FTP (for "file transfer protocol") to download files to your computer. Plus, you needed a browser to view (or browse through) the graphical portion of the Internet known as the Web. Now all those functions are built into browsers.

Keep Your Browser Current to Keep Your Computer Secure Hardly a month goes by without someone finding a new security hole in a popular browser and its maker quickly plugging it. Keep your Web browser current—and your e-mail software too—by visiting the Web sites of their makers regularly and downloading any security patches or new versions. *Be sure you download those only from their makers' Web sites.* There have been reports of people receiving e-mail containing "security patches" for Microsoft products that were actually hacker code to steal passwords. You can find out what version of Netscape you have by pulling down the **Help** menu and selecting **About Communicator**. If it's less than 4.5, you should download a new version from Netscape's Web site (**http://www.netscape.com**). If you're running Internet Explorer, from the **Help** menu, select About **Internet Explorer**. If you're running a version prior to 5.0, you should download a new copy from Microsoft's Web site (**http://www.microsoft.com**).

Most computers are sold with Netscape's Navigator or Microsoft's Internet Explorer already installed. You can also download them for free from **Netscape** (**http://www.netscape.com**) or **Microsoft** (**http://www.microsoft.com**).

While you can use just about any computer to log onto the Internet in some fashion (even an original Apple II, circa 1979), to be able to view graphics you'll need a computer manufactured in at least the last 8 years. If you have an older computer download a copy of the $35 **Opera** browser (**http://www.opera.com**), which will run on any PCs running Windows 3.x—even ones as old as 386SX's with 6 megabytes of RAM.

If you're running an older Macintosh, head to Chris Adams' **Web Browsers for Antique Macs** Web page (**http://www.edprint.demon.co.uk/se/macweb.html**) and download Tradewave's MacWeb or an early version of NCSA Mosaic.

If you've never configured Internet software before, you'll need someone to help you, even if you're a computer genius (believe us, we know). Your ISP will (or should) give you directions on how to set up Windows 95 or the Macintosh OS to at least log on to their service. But once you're connected, you're pretty much on your own. That's why we've put together this little tutorial.

Note: The following directions are for the latest versions of Explorer and Navigator, but, with the exception of the instructions for e-mail, most will work with earlier versions of the browsers.

HOW TO TAP INTO A WEB PAGE

© Jim and Gloria Winer

To get to a Web page, such as Mimi Winer's **Everything for Dollmaking**, type its address (also known as its URL, or "Uniform Resource Locator") into the **Address**: bar in Navigator or the **Location**: bar in Internet Explorer

Take note that the case of the letters is important.

You can also cut and paste URLs from other documents into the address or location bar. Highlight the address with your mouse, press **Ctrl-C** (⌘-C on a Mac), then place the mouse in the location bar and press **Ctrl-V** (⌘-V on a Mac) to paste it in. Then hit **<ENTER>**.

To move to other pages in the Web site, click on highlighted words, or, when your mouse is over a link (demonstrated by the cursor changing into a hand when positioned over an object), right-click your mouse to follow the link.

How to Find the Web Site
if the Web Page Isn't There

URLs point you to directories on a remote computer just as directory paths (c:\windows\programs) get you to different directories and subdirectories on your computer's hard disk. If a Web address doesn't get you to what you want, try working back through theURL. For example, Denise Van Patten, the doll collecting guide at **About.Com**, offers an article about how to get started making porcelain dolls at this long-winded

URL: **http://collectdolls.about.com/hobbies/collectdolls/library/weekly/aa110999.htm**

If the article doesn't appear when you type this into your browser, trying going backward one step to:

http://collectdolls.about.com/hobbies/collectdolls/library/weekly

If there's nothing there, or if you get a weird error message, try working back through the URL to the domain name at:

http://collectdolls.about.com

If you're working back through a URL and get you to a directory that lists files like this, you can click on the highlighted names to view or even download them. If you see a file with an "HTM" or "HTML" at the end of its name, click on it. That's a Web page document. If it has a ".GIF" or ".JPG" extension, it's a picture. If you get an

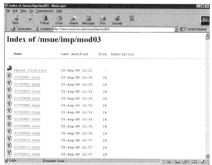

error message like "Access denied," try going further back through the URL. This is a directory for the Web site of the Michigan State University Extension where you can find all sorts of pamphlets on home and textiles topics.

What does all that gobbledygook in a URL mean?

The http: tells your Internet service what kind of document you are trying to access on the Internet. HTTP stands for "hyper-text transfer protocol," the protocol of the Web. You might run into ftp:, which stands for "file transfer protocol," an early Internet scheme for transferring files. The protocol is always followed by //, which separates it from the document's address.

Next comes the domain name, such as www.ctpub.com. The triple-w designates C&T's Web subdirectory on its Internet server. The .com suffix indicates that C&T is a commercial entity. If C&T were a university it would have an .edu suffix; if it were a nonprofit, it would have a .org. The words that following the domain name, separated by slashes, designate further subdirectories. Many, though not all, URLs end with a specific file name.

COMMON ERROR MESSAGES WHEN YOU ENTER A WEB ADDRESS

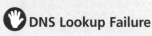 **404 Not Found**
The requested URL /blocks/tips.html was not found on this server.

Reason: Your browser was able to find the Internet service or the computer on which the Web site was or is hosted, but no such page was found on the service. (The very last word "word" at the end of a URL is the page's address. In this example, it's **tips.html**.) Maybe the Web site owner removed that particular page, or perhaps the Web site no longer exists.
Fix: Try working back through the URL, as explained in the above tip on page 19, to see if you can locate the Web site or determine if the site itself is gone from the service. Also, try suffixing the page's address with "htm" or "html" instead of its current extension. For example, in place of **TIPS.HTML**, type **TIPS.HTM**. (An HTML suffix is the same as an HTM, but some Web page hosting services require that Web pages be named with one or the other. Typing the wrong extension is a common mistake.)

DNS Lookup Failure
or
Unable to locate the server.
The server does not have a DNS entry.

Reason: DNS stands for "domain name server." A domain name is the first part of a URL—for instance, in **www.ctpub.com**, ctpub.com is the domain name. Every Internet service (and AOL) has a database of such Web page host addresses. When you type a URL, the first thing your browser does is tell your Internet service to look up the domain name in its database to find out where it's located. If it can't find it, your Internet service's computer may poll other domain name directories around the Internet to determine if any of them know where the domain name can be found. If none of them do, you may get the error message "DNS Lookup Failure."

Why can't they find the domain name? Maybe it no longer exists. Or perhaps it's so new that the domain name databases your Internet service uses can't find it. Sometimes you also get this error message when there's heavy traffic on the Internet. Your Internet service is taking too long to look up the name, so your browser errors out.

Fix: Try typing the URL into your browser later in the day. If you still get the error message, try the URL a few days, even a week later. If you still get error messages, the domain name no longer exists.

No Response from Server

Reason: Your browser is unable to get a timely response from the Web site's host computer. This can because of heavy traffic, either on the Internet as a whole or on the branch of the Internet you are traveling. It can be because the computer that's hosting the Web site is overloaded from too many people tapping in. Or it can be because your Internet service is overloaded, or its own computers are experiencing slowdowns for technical reasons.

Fix: Try the URL again, either in a few minutes or later in the day.

Server Is Busy

Reason: A common error message issued by Barbie.Com and other heavily trafficked doll sites, this message means that too many people are trying to tap in.

Fix: Try accessing the Web site later.

![bear icon] FIND YOUR WAY AROUND THE WEB WITHOUT GETTING LOST

Right-click on the **Back** button in your browser for a list of Web sites you've recently visited. Click on their names to return to them.

• Click the **Back** button in your browser to return to previously visited Web sites.

• Click the **History** button or select the history feature from a drop-down menu to list previously visited URLs.

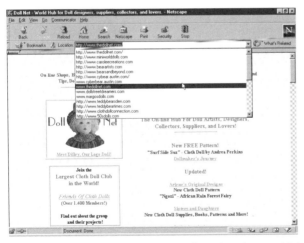

Click your browser's drop-down location box, which displays the last dozen or so URLs that you have actually typed into the browser (in other words, it doesn't display links that you've clicked on something to get to).

HOW TO USE BOOKMARKS

To add a bookmark to Explorer, click **Favorites/Add to Favorites**. *You can also drag URLs to the Link toolbar to create buttons. Display the links toolbar by heading to* **View/Toolbars/Links**.

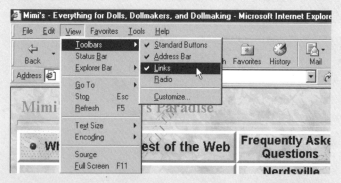

Web browsers let you "bookmark" sites so that you can visit them again simply by fishing through your bookmark catalog. You usually just click a bookmark icon (or Favorites in Internet Explorer) or select the feature from a toolbar to add the Web site that you're currently visiting to your bookmark list.

While a Web page is displayed right click on the page and, from the pop-up menu, select **Add Bookmark**.

You Can Add Shortcuts to Web Sites on Your Windows Desktop. Say there's a particular Web site you like to visit every day. If you're running Windows 95/98, you can add a shortcut to it from your desktop. When you click on the shortcut, your browser will load, dial your Internet service, and speed you to the Web site. Use your mouse to drag the site's URL to the desktop from a link in a Web page. Or, if you're using Internet Explorer, drag from the **Address** bar to the left of the Links bar or the **Favorites** menu. If you're using Netscape, drag the icon to the left of **Location**: when a page is loaded. Your mouse cursor should change into a circle with a slash as you drag the URL to the desktop.

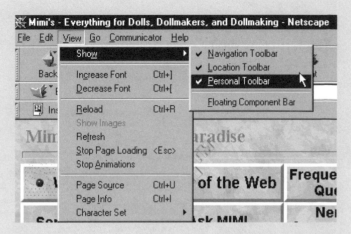

Create buttons on your personal toolbar in Netscape to whiz you to the Web sites you like to visit frequently. First, display the toolbar by pulling down the **View** menu, selecting **Show**, and placing a check beside **Personal Toolbar**.

Then, while the Web page is displayed, drag the **Location** icon to the **Personal Toolbar** just below.

The icon should look like this when you're successfully dragging the Web site's location to your toolbar.

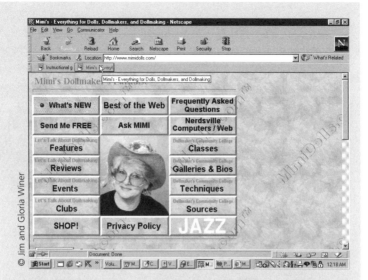

Mimi's - Everything for Dolls, Dollmakers, and Dollmaking - Netscape

File   Edit   View   Go   Communicator   Help

Back   Reload   Home   Search   Netscape   Print   Security   Stop

Bookmarks   Location: http://www.mimidolls.com/

Instructional g   Mimi's

Jim and Gloria Winer

Click this button in the **Personal Toolbar** *whenever you want your browser to take you to Mimi's Dollmaker's Paradise.*

You Can Customize Your Browser's Personal Toolbar by Adding Bookmarks.

You can customize the personal toolbar in Communicator or the **Links** bar in Internet Explorer by adding not only icons for frequently visited URLs but also folders of bookmarks. In Communicator, add a URL to the personal toolbar by dragging a link from a Web page or by dragging the icon to the left of **Location**: when a page is loaded. To add a folder to the personal toolbar, click the **Bookmarks** icon, select **Edit Bookmarks**, and highlight the folder you wish to place on the toolbar. Right-click and select **Set as Toolbar Folder**. In Internet Explorer, you can similarly customize the **Links** bar by adding folders as well as individual URLs. Drag folders from the **Favorites** menu to add them to the **Links** bar. To add a URL to the link bar, drag it from the **Address** bar to the left of the **Links** bar, from the **Favorites** menu, or from a Web page.

You Can Use Third-Party Bookmark Software to Organize Your Bookmarks.

You can download a lot of low-cost utilities for organizing bookmarks from the Web. These are particularly handy if you're using two browsers—both Netscape and Internet Explorer, for example. They enable you to store your bookmarks in a central location and organize them into folders with icons in a more efficient manner than you can in your browser. Some utilities also let you password protect bookmarks. A good spot from which to download them is C/net's **Shareware.Com** (**http://www.shareware.com**). Search for the phrase "bookmark organizer." For PCs, one we like is the $29 shareware program LinkMan Professional from Thomas Reimann. For Macs, we like URL Manager Pro, the $25 shareware program from **Alco Blom** (**http://www.url-manager.com**).

Can't Find a Picture That You've Saved to Your Disk? It happens all the time. You click on an image on the Web to save it to your computer, then you can't find it. If you can't remember the name of the graphic that you saved, go back to the Web page and click on it again to see the name. Then, if you have a PC running Windows 95/98/2000, click **Start**, then click **Find**, and finally type the name of the file. Windows will find it for you. On a Macintosh, click the **Apple** Menu and select Sherlock. Type the file name in the search box, and Sherlock will find it for you.

If You Can't Access a Web Page Try These Tricks:

• If Netscape's logo keeps "snowing" but doesn't display any page, it may be because Netscape has frozen. Try accessing the Web site with Explorer instead. For convenience, cut the URL from Netscape's **Location** bar and paste it into Explorer's.

• If you click on a highlighted link on a Web page but don't seem to go anywhere, try right-clicking on the link instead. From the pop up box, select "Open in New Window" or "Open Frame In New Window."

• If you click to a Web page with Netscape and the Web page appears to be blank, try accessing it with Explorer instead. Netscape is fussy about certain types of coding on pages and may refuse to load a page because it choked on a less-than-perfect piece of coding.

• If a page doesn't appear to load properly, click the **Reload** button.

• If you're running Internet Explorer 5 and occasionally Web pages load only partially, you need to download a patch from Microsoft's Web site (**http://www.microsoft.com**).

PRINTING WEB PAGES AND SAVING PICTURES TO DISK

When you're surfing the Web you're often going to want to print a page or save a picture of it to your disk to examine later.

To Print a Web Page

From your browser's menu, select **Print**. If the page has frames, you may need to first click on the frame that you want to print in order to select it. From the **File** menu, select **Page Setup** if you want to print the URL or date on the page (this feature is available only in newer browsers).

To Save a Picture to Disk

Position your cursor over the image and right-click. (On a Mac, click-and-hold.) A menu box will pop up. Select **Save Image As**... or **Save Picture As**.... You can view it later, either in your browser or in a graphics program such as Paint Shop Pro.

Judy & Gloria's Ten-Step Program for Fixing Browser and Graphics Crashes

After you spend an hour or so clicking around decorating Web sites your browser may start acting flaky. Maybe Web pages stop appearing so quickly or your computer grinds its disk a lot. Maybe your PC just locks up. Any number of things could be causing the problem. Follow these steps to help keep your browser and computer crash-free:

STEP 1. Cold boot the PC. In other words, shut down your software, turn the power off, and turn it back on a few minutes later when the disk stops spinning. That will clean any flotsam out of its memory. Your browser will be flying again when you log back on the Web, but this solution is only temporary. Some people reboot their PC several times in the course of an evening. We think that's unnecessary. That's why we recommend the following steps.

STEP 2. Head to the Web sites of the makers of your PC, its video card, and its modem, and download any fixes or new drivers.

STEP 3. Clean up your hard disk by running Scandisk and Disk Defragmenter. Click **Start/Programs/Accessories/System Tools**. (You should do this every few weeks.)

STEP 4. If you're running Windows 95/98/2000, head to Microsoft's Web site (**http://www.microsoft.com**) and download any new fixes, patches, or upgrades. (There are always fixes to download for Windows.) While you're there, download the current version of Internet Explorer and any fixes for that too, if it's the browser you run. If you use Netscape, get the newest version (**http://www.netscape.com**).

STEP 5. If you're running a version of AOL 3.0 earlier than 131.75, you need to upgrade. For AOL 4.0, upgrade if its version number is lower than 134.224. If you're running Windows 95 and experiencing crashes with AOL 5.0 or 4.0, you might want to return to using AOL 3.0. Use the keyword **upgrade**. To find out what version of AOL you're running, click **Help/About America Online**. Hit **Ctrl-R** when the AOL window pops up.

STEP 6. A surfing browser will push your computer's memory to the limit. Try shutting down unnecessary applications while surfing and see if that helps. Press **Ctrl-Alt-Delete** to get a list of applications and close down everything but Explorer, Systray, and your browser. To troubleshoot your system further, right-click on **My Computer** and choose **Properties**. In the **Device Manager** tab, make sure that no red or yellow flags signal hardware conflicts. In the **Performance** tab, make sure that System Resources scores at least 85% free. Click the **Virtual Memory** button and select "Let Windows manager my virtual memory settings." Click OK. If AOL's crashing, you should try shutting down your virus software to see if that might be the source of the conflict.

STEP 7. Your browser needs lots of disk space for caching. At least 50 megabytes or 10 percent of your disk should be free. You should empty your browser's cache weekly. Delete Netscape's history file (netscape.hst) and Cache folder. Clean out AOL's cache by heading to **My AOL/Preferences/WWW**. Head to the **General** tab and click the **Delete Files** and **Clear History** buttons. For Explorer, delete the folder Temporary Internet Files, found in the Window directory.

STEP 8. If Web page pictures look smeary or if your computer locks up while you're scrolling down a page, your video driver or graphics card may be at fault. Right-click on an empty spot in the desktop, then click **Properties**. In the **Settings** tab, change the **Colors** to 256. Click **Apply**. Under the **Performance** tab, move down the **Hardware Acceleration** slider a notch. Click OK.

STEP 9. If your browser crashes while printing Web pages, it may be because your printer needs an updated driver. Or, it might need a bidirectional cable. Most printers are sold with bidirectional cables these days, but there's always that odd duck. But try this first: head to the Control Panel, click the **Printer** icon, then right-click on the icon for your printer. Select **Properties**. In the **Details** tab, select **Spool Settings**. Set it to "Print direct to printer." If there's an option to disable bi-directional support, do it.

STEP 10. If you think Netscape is at fault, head to Netscape's crash troubleshooting page (**http://help.netscape.com/kb/client/970203-1.html**). If you think Explorer is at fault, write down the Invalid Page Fault error message it spits out, then search for the message on Microsoft's tech support site (**http://www.microsoft.com/support**). Better yet, search for the names of your computer, your graphics card, and your modem on *both* Web sites. The chances are very good that you'll find your solution on one of them.

Here are more things to try:

• If you're feeling ambitious, download a new version of your browser, then uninstall your old one (this step is important). Finally, reinstall the new one.

• If Explorer spits out a Java or ActiveX error while trying to display a Web site, then goes belly up, try disabling these scripting languages. From the **Tools** menu, select **Internet Options**. Head to the **Security** tab and click the **Internet** icon. Click dots beside Disable in these categories: Download signed ActiveX controls, Run ActiveX controls and plugins, Active Scripting, and Scripting of Java applets. Under **Java**, select **Disable Java**.

• If AOL is the source of your woes (the sign that the problem lays with your AOL software and not too many people logging on to the AOL network is that AOL freezes without the hourglass symbol), try deleting the AOL Adapter. From the **Start** menu, select **Settings**, then **Control Panel**. Click the **Network** icon and head to the **Configuration** tab. Highlight "AOL Adapter" and click **Remove**. Restart Windows. Sign back on to AOL and AOL will reinstall an updated version of the adapter.

• Try calling a different AOL number and see if that remedies the freeze-ups. Head to **My AOL/Access Numbers** to find a new number.

• Use the keywords **Help Community** to find up-to-date solutions to AOL freeze-ups.

Mac User Alert! If AOL crashes repeatedly, a corrupt AOL Preferences file in the System Folder may be to blame. To trash AOL's preferences file, first quit AOL. Then open **System Folder/Preferences/ AOL/Preferences**. *Drag only the* **AOL Preferences** *file to the trash. Relaunch AOL's software. AOL's software will create a new preferences file in the System File.*

![bear icon] HOW TO SEND E-MAIL

If you're using America Online, all you need to do is click on the You Have Mail icon on the greeting screen to read your e-mail or send mail, even out on the Internet. (To send messages to someone on the Internet from AOL, type the full Internet address—for example, **info@ctpub.com**—into the **To**: line in the AOL mail screen, just as you'd type an AOL address.)

If you're using an Internet service you can use special mail software such as Eudora or Pegasus. Or, you can use the mail program built into your browser.

In Navigator, press **Ctrl-2** to get to Messenger, the mail program. On a Mac, click the **Mail** icon box in the lower-right hand corner of the browser's screen to get to your in-box; ⌘-T retrieves new e-mail.

In Explorer, click the **Mail** icon in your Windows 95/98 tray to load the Outlook Express mail program.

![bear icon] HOW TO READ USENET NEWSGROUPS WITH YOUR WEB BROWSER

Many talk groups for doll lovers swirl through that raucous amalgam of newsgroups known as Usenet. But tapping into them can be tricky. You need to set up your browser to download the groups from your Internet service, then use your browser's mail reader to read them.

The first time you want to read a newsgroup you'll need to download a complete list of current newsgroups from your ISP. You'll then need to search it and subscribe to the groups you're interested in. Finally, you need to download the messages themselves. Here's how to do it with Netscape and Explorer:

![hand icon] **Warning!** The Usenet newsgroups are unmoderated and uncensored. We've spotted a lot of pornography in some of the newsgroups.

How to Read the Usenet Doll Making and Collecting Newsgroups with Netscape

1. You must first set up your browser to retrieve newsgroups from your Internet server. Find out from your Internet service the name of the computer where newgroups are stored. (It will be something like **groups.myisp.com**.) Pull down the **Edit** menu and select **Preferences**. Under **Mail & Newsgroups**, head to the **Newsgroup Servers** or **Group Server** setup box and click **Add**. Type the name of your ISP's newsgroup server. Click OK to save it.

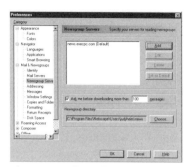

First you need to tell Navigator the name of the server on your ISP where newsgroups are stored.

2. Connect to your Internet service.

3. Head to Navigator's message center by pressing **Ctrl-2** (click the **Mail** icon box in the lower-right hand corner of the browser's screen on a Mac).

4. From the **File** menu, select **Subscribe to Discussion Groups**.

5. Click the **All** or **All Groups** tab to download a list of current newsgroups. This may take a while, since the list is large. The message "Receiving discussion groups" should appear on the very bottom line of the screen. Hit the **Refresh List** button if you or someone else in your household have set up the newsreader to subscribe to mailing lists in the past.

You need to download the complete list of newsgroups in order to search for the ones you're interested in.

6. When that humongous list of newsgroups has finished downloading, head to the **Search for a Group** tab. Type "doll" or "craft" (or one of the newsgroup names listed in the table on page 39) in the search box and click the **Search Now** button.

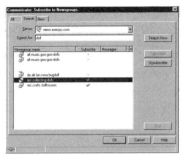

Search for the newsgroup list by heading to the search tab. After you've located newsgroups you'd like to read, subscribe to them by selecting them. You can click through the list just as you'd click through subdirectories on your computer.

7. Once the newsgroup searcher has come up with a list of interesting newsgroups, highlight the one you want to read, and press the **Subscribe** button. A check will appear beside it.

8. To read your newsgroup, head back to the message center (**Ctrl-2**, or click the **Mail** icon box on a Mac). From the pulldown menu box at the top of the screen, select the newsgroup and click **Download Messages** or the **Get Msg** icon. You may want to download only a selection (under 500 for example) and mark the rest of the messages as read. This way, the next time you download messages from the newsgroup, you will only download the newest ones.

Select the messages and message threads you want to read and they'll appear in the bottom of the screen. (If you don't get a split screen you may need to "pull up" the bottom portion of the screen with your mouse. In other words, the window is there, it's just hidden.)

9. From the **Go** menu you can move from thread to thread, reading some messages and skipping others.

10. To read messages in the future, go to the message center (**Ctrl-2**, or click the **Mail** icon box on a Mac). From the pulldown menu box at the top of the screen, select the newsgroup you want to read. From the **File** menu, select **Get**

Messages/New.

How to Read the Usenet Doll Making and Collecting Newsgroups with Microsoft Explorer

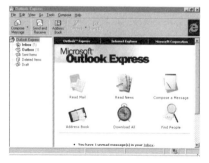

1. Load the Outlook Express mail portion of Internet Explorer by clicking on the mailbox icon on the top right-hand corner of the screen. Click the **Read**

News icon on the Express screen. If you have not yet set it up to read newsgroups with your ISP, a setup wizard will appear. It will prompt you for your name, e-mail address, and the name of the dial-up connection you use to connect to your ISP. Most important of all, it will ask you the name of the server on your ISP where the news messages can be found.

2. The next time you click Express's **Read News** icon, it will ask you if you'd like to download a list of the newsgroups from your ISP. This may take a while since there are tens of thousands of newsgroups.

3. Type "doll" to search the list for newsgroups that contain "doll" in their name, or type in names of newsgroups from the table on page 39. Subscribe to them by highlighting each, then clicking the **Subscribe** button. Click OK when you're done.

4. To read newsgroups that you've subscribed to, click the **Go To** button or click on the name of the newsgroup on the left side of the screen. To read individual messages, click on the headers displayed at the top right of the screen.

Warning! If you try to download more than about 500 newsgroup messages with Explorer, it will crash.

How to Read the Usenet Doll Making and Collecting Newsgroups on America Online

1. To read the Internet newsgroups through AOL, press **Ctrl-K** (⌘-K on a Mac) and type the keyword NEWSGROUPS. Click the **Search All Newsgroups** icon to search the tens of thousands of newsgroups for ones in your interests.

2. When AOL comes up with a list of matching newsgroups, click on the name of the newsgroup and, from the pop-up box, click "Subscribe to newsgroup." Depending upon which version of AOL's software you're using, you may be able to read the messages in the newly subscribed newsgroup immediately or you may need to head back to the main newsgroup menu by closing the windows (click the X in the upper right-hand corner). Click the **Read My Newsgroups** button to pop up a list of the newsgroups to which you're subscribed. Click the **List Unread** button to list messages in the newsgroups that you have not yet read.

3. To read listed messages click the title of the message.

Usenet Newsgroups Where You'll Find Doll and Teddy Making and Collecting Discussions

rec.crafts.misc	Discuss just about any craft
rec.crafts.dollhouses	Talk about dollhouses and dolls
rec.crafts.textiles.quilting	Anything having to do with quilting
rec.crafts.textiles.needlework	Any form of hand-stitching is discussed
rec.crafts.textiles.sewing	Sewing clothes, furnishings, etc.
rec.crafts.textiles.yarn	Any craft involved with yarn
rec.crafts.textiles.misc	Miscellaneous fiber and textile discussions
rec.crafts.polymer-clay	For fans of the fantastic clay
rec.crafts.marketplace	Small ads for craft products
alt.crafts. professional	A forum for craft professionals
bit.listserv.clayart	For fans of pottery and ceramics
uk.rec.crafts	Hobnob with United Kingdom crafters
rec.toys.vintage	A discussion group for antique toy afficianadoes
rec.collecting.dolls	A favorite hang-out for doll fans
alt.collecting.teddy-bears	Discuss teddy bear collecting
rec.toys.misc	Discuss toy collecting

TIPS FOR STAYING SAFE ON THE WEB

The Internet is safer than the average subway station—but sometimes not by much. We know you're an adult and will take care of yourself, just as you would in a subway station. But just so you know we're concerned about your safety, here are our motherly warnings:

• Never give anyone your credit card number, any of your online passwords, or any personal information, including your street address or phone number. An all-too-common ruse is for hackers to e-mail a new sub-scriber to America Online alleging, that they are a rep-resentative of AOL and need the subscriber to resubmit their credit card number for verification. Another ploy is for hackers to claim they work for Microsoft and to e-mail victims a "security patch" for Internet Explorer. Once the "security patch" is installed, it e-mails the vic-tim's passwords to the hackers. No one ever e-mails a security patch!

• Don't open any file attachment that comes with an e-mail message from a stranger. This is how viruses and Trojan horse programs (programs which snatch your passwords or do nasty things to your computer) are sent. Also, if you're on AOL, don't click on any hyper-links or Web addresses that arrive in your mailbox from a stranger.

• Beware of get-rich-quick offers that arrive by the megabyte in your e-mail box. And never answer junk e-mail. You'll be bombarded with more e-mail, and the sender may retaliate if you ask to be removed from their mailing list.

- If you shop on the Web, pay with a credit card in case there are problems. Never type your credit card into any Web site that's not a "secure" Web site, meaning that the site will encrypt the information you send. As you enter a secure site, your browser will tell you that it's secure, and Navigator will display a lock icon.

- Be sure to supervise your children on the Net—the best way is to talk to them regularly about what they're doing online. Warn them as often as you can not to meet in person strangers they've met online, even if they insist the new friend is a teenager—sometimes they're not.

- Keep the kids away from the Usenet newsgroups, where pornography is rife. If you're on AOL use the Parental Controls (keywords **parental controls**) to block your child's access to Usenet. You should also block their screen name from receiving binary files (including pictures) in e-mail.

Read Doll and Teddy Newsgroups from Your Browser
You can read newsgroups from the comfort of your Web browser by heading to Deja.Com (**http://www.deja.com/usenet**). Reading them through this Web site isn't as easy as reading them with your browser's newsreader, but it's a simple way to access the groups.

free Big Web Sites for Doll Makers

There are literally thousands of Web pages by and for doll makers on the Internet. But there are just a few sites where doll makers congregate. On these mega-sites, you'll find free patterns, tutorials, links to the Web sites of many doll makers, and, of course, lots of good doll-related conversation. If you're new to the Web, we recommend starting by visiting the sites in this chapter.

 ## CLOTHART
http://www.martydoll.com/index.html

Marty Donnellan's Web site offers tips and techniques, a mailing list for doll artists, a gallery of dolls, and some hard-to-find supplies for doll makers.

 ## AUNTIE.COM
http://www.auntie.com

Auntie's site offers occasional articles on doll-making, plus patterns and regular features on dolls, doll history, and collecting.

Everink maintains a large directory of doll and bear-related Web sites (**http://www.everink.com/ndl.html**). This is a great Web site to search for special tools, as well as the Web sites of other doll makers who specialize in the sort of doll making that you enjoy.

THE CLOTH DOLL CONNECTION
http://www.clothdollconnection.com

Karen Samuelson's Cloth Doll Connection is a fabulous site where you'll find doll-making tips, links to free doll-making patterns all over the Web, a mailing list, book reviews, and much more.

🛒 DOLL NET
http://www.thedollnet.com

All doll-making in cyberspace points toward Doll Net, where you'll find recommendations about shopping for doll-making supplies on the Web, free doll patterns, bulletin boards, chats, a mailing list, a gallery of dolls crafted by other cyber doll makers, and much more.

 **DOLL STREET DREAMERS**
http://www.dollstreetdreamers.com

Molly Finnegan's clever and witty site serves as cyber depot to doll makers who just want to have fun making dolls. You'll find the Doll Street Dreams Doll Club, the Chatterer's Cafe & Carwash, the Doll Street Gazette, and more.

🛒 MIMI'S DOLL MAKER'S PARADISE
http://www.mimidolls.com

Jim and Gloria J. "Mimi" Winer run this marvelous site, which includes lots of doll photos, gossip on the professional world of doll making, and links to all the good doll crafting stuff on the Web. You'll also find Mimi's doll maker's handbook, which is a treasure trove of good advice and direction.

free Big Web Sites for Doll Collectors

Whether you collect Barbies, Raggedy Anns, or American Girl dolls, there are Web sites out there that will encourage you to collect more. They'll help you identify your dolls, they'll tell you how to re-root their hair, and they'll tell you how to starch their pinafores to keep them looking pristine. They'll also put you in touch with other doll collectors and help you to determine the value of your collection.

DOLL COLLECTING AT ABOUT.COM
http://collectdolls.about.com

Denise Van Patten leads you to all the best Web sites for collecting vinyl, cloth, porcelain, and paper dolls. She includes a great section on restoration and repair advice. She offers display advice and much more. This should be your first stop if you're a doll collector!

KAYLEE'S KORNER — THE DOLL COLLECTION CONNECTION
http://www.dollinfo.com/index.html

There are message boards for doll collectors, an e-mail newsletter, a doll of the month, lots of advice and fun, and a huge directory of Web resources about dolls.

DOLL COLLECTING AT COLLECTOR'S UNIVERSE
http://www.collectors.com/dolls

Collector's Universe offers some captivating articles on dolls, plus price guides and a guide to shows around the country.

BEGINNER'S GUIDE TO ACTION FIGURE COLLECTING
http://www.toymania.com/beginnersguide

Learn the ten rules of acquisition, read a collector's crash course, discover toy tracking tactics, and more from Eric G. Myers, Jason A. Geyer, and the Raving Toy Mania.

GARY'S TIPS ON DOLL COLLECTING
http://www.sowatzka.com/gary/tips.htm

Gary Sowatzka tells you how to get started collecting dolls. He tells you about different sorts of vintage dolls, including composition, bisque, French bisque, German bisque, glazed china heads, untinted bisque, paper mache, and wax dolls. He even offers advice on how to ship dolls.

TOY COLLECTING AT ABOUT.COM
http://toycollecting.about.com

Gianfranco Origliato is your guide to price guides, features, links to discussion groups about Japanese toys, bears, Beanies, Furbies, Star Wars figures, and more.

DOLL COLLECTING FROM SUITE 101
http://www.suite101.com/welcome.cfm/doll_collecting

Karen Ledbetter writes monthly articles and leads you to lots of good stuff on the Net for doll collectors.

THE BIG RED TOYBOX
http://www.bigredtoybox.com

Among the marvels on this huge Web site for toy collectors is a "toy locator" database into which you can type the type of toy and select the manufacturer. The site will tell you what it thinks the toy is. It will then display classifieds from collectors who'd like to buy that type of toy. You'll also find a database containing pictures of different vintage toys, particularly dolls and action figures, as well as descriptions.

KIDS COLLECTING AT ABOUT.COM
http://www.kidscollecting.about.com

Robert Olson is your guide to collecting Pokéman, American Girls, Beanies, bears, yo-yos, Boy Scout merit badges, and more.

VICKY'S HOME ON THE NET
http://www.vicky-web.com

Vicky in Florida maintains this treasure trove of information and advice for doll collectors. There's doll news and collectors' gossip, plus links to other relevant information on the Net.

 *More Web Sites for Doll Collectors*

MAD ABOUT THAT DOLL—AN EDUCATIONAL RESOURCE FOR DOLL COLLECTORS
http://home.flash.net/~dsquard7/newsflash.html

Read the latest news and gossip about your favorite dolls.

WEB OF DOLLS—DOLL COLLECTING OP ED AND OTHER OPINIONS
http://www.cyberramp.com/~lfurlet/index.html

Linda Furlet collects many different types of dolls. She offers sassy opinions on her favorite collectibles.

Are Barbie Collectors Low Class? (Not in Our Opinion!)
http://www.cyberramp.com/~lfurlet/barbie/class.htm

Questions to Ask Sellers About Dolls
http://www.cyberramp.com/~lfurlet/madame/sellers.htm

Doll (Barbie) Collecting Lies
http://www.cyberramp.com/~lfurlet/barbie/lies.htm

Excuses to Buy a Doll
http://www.cyberramp.com/~lfurlet/madame/excuses.htm

FASHIONABLE LADIES: THE ONLINE ENCYCLOPEDIA OF GLAMOUR DOLLS, 1955-1964
http://www.fashionable-ladies.litchfield.nh.us

Zendelle Bouchard maintains this guide to glamour dolls such as Madame Alexander, Twixie, and Little Miss Ginger.

DOLL FINDER
http://www.dollfinder.com

Visit Doll News for the latest information on doll collecting.

 **🛒 KATY'S KOLLECTIBLES**
http://www.katyskollectibles.com

Read articles about doll collecting, visit chat rooms, and tap into bulletin board discussions.

SMALL WALKING DOLLS OF THE 1950'S
http://50sdolls.com

Nancy Kerson's step-by-step guide will to help you identify the "Ginny-type" dolls made in the 1950's.

 A DOLL'S HOUSE
http://www.scican.net/~sdecker/main.html

Shari Decker is working on an online museum devoted to dolls of the '50s. She also hosts an e-mail list for collectors and a bulletin board.

 *Hunting for a Certain Doll?* If you're shopping for a limited edition or one-of-a-kind doll by a popular doll artist, visit All Doll Gallery (**http://www.alldolls.com**). You'll find links to the Web sites of well-known doll artists. You should also check out Antique Doll.Com (**http://www.antiquedoll.com**), DollMasters (**http://www.dollmasters.com**), and Doll Menagerie (**http://www.dollmenagerie.com**).

 ## THE DOLL PAGE
http://www.dollpage.com

Read doll news and feature articles. In addition to being a very large online source of dolls, this site includes doll news and articles, and will soon contain doll show information. Click Fun Stuff for bulletin boards and a chat room.

Web Sites for Collectors of Specific Sorts of Dolls

No matter what kind of doll you collect, there's probably a Web site or two devoted to it. Here's a selection of some of our favorite sites to devoted to specific collectible dolls.

GENE LOVERS UNITE
http://www.cybcon.com/~toad/glu.htm

Are you a fan of Gene dolls? You'll love this site, which includes news, photos and lots of links to other Web resources.

DENI'S VINTAGE BARBIE
http://www.dolls4play.com

Denise Davidson shows you her collection and helps you determine which doll you have and when it was manufactured.

RAGGEDY LAND
http://www.raggedyland.com

If you're a collector of Raggedy Ann and Andy, head to this Web site where you can read news, chat with other collectors, tap into other Raggedy-related Web pages, and read features and FAQs about your favorite doll.

CANDI GIRLS
http://agnes.dida.physik.uni-essen.de/~anja/candi.html

Candi Girl fashion dolls have some unusual qualities, such as bendable legs. Introduced in 1996, the dolls have unique ethnic face molds, including ones for African-American, Asian, Hispanic, Danish, and Swedish dolls. Anja Drewitz tells you all about the dolls, including their history, and leads you to other related information about them on the Web.

ANNA'S STRAWBERRY SHORTCAKE COLLECTOR'S SITE
http://www.angelfire.com/hi/sscake

Strawberry Shortcake fans will appreciate the information on this site, which includes cleaning tips for these sometimes hard-to-clean dolls.

BARBIE DOLL COLLECTING AT ABOUT.COM
http://barbiedolls.about.com

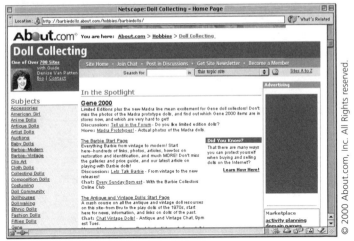

Sarah Locker is your host for weekly articles, a newsletter, a chat room for Barbie loves, and lots of links to other Web resources devoted to America's favorite doll.

MATTEL'S BARBIE.COM
http://www.barbie.com/collectors

Mattel's official collecting site includes fun facts, tips and glossary, frequently asked questions, and collector terminology—for instance, "NRFB" means "never removed from box."

THE MIDGE PAGE
http://home.flash.net/~dsquard7/aboutmidge.html

Barbie's first friend was Midge Hadley, introduced to the market in 1963. Learn all about Midge and how she changed over the years.

KEEPING KEN
http://www.manbehindthedoll.com

Do you love Ken? This site is devoted to Barbie's hunk. You'll find a valuation guide and lots of other information.

THE ORIGINAL CHATTY CATHY'S COLLECTOR'S CLUB
http://www.ttinet.com/chattycathy

Melissa Gilkey Mince tells you about Chatty Cathy and helps you figure out what yours might be worth.

MADAME ALEXANDER
http://www.alexanderdoll.com

This is the official site for Madame Alexander dolls. There's a collectors' forum and a doll hospital with tips on how to care for your dolls.

LEGENDARY BEAUTIES—THE DOLLS OF MADAME ALEXANDER®
http://www.cyberramp.net/~lfurlet/madame

There's news for collectors, trading boards, advise on cleaning dolls, and hints for those who plan to sell their dolls.

MADAME ALEXANDER DOLL CLUB
http://www.madc.org

THE AMERICAN GIRLS COLLECTION
http://www.americangirl.com/catalogue/agcollection.html

On this official Web site for American Girls from the Pleasant Company, you'll learn about upcoming dolls and related products.

THE DOLLIKIN COLLECTOR'S GROUP
http://home.att.net/~dollikin/dollikin.html

Learn how to identify, restore and repair your Dollikins.

THE OFFICIAL HOME OF BEANIE BABIES
http://www.ty.com

Head to Ty's Web site to learn the latest about your favorite floppy dolls and talk to other Beanie fans.

Bulletin Boards for Doll Collectors

There are many Web sites where you can chat bulletin-board style with other doll collectors. To join the conversation, all you need do is point your browser toward the discussion group's URL. The advantage of Web discussion boards, as opposed to chat rooms or mailing lists, is that messages tend to hang around for a long time. The drawback is that discussions tend not to be as lively as those found in mailing lists.

ANTIQUE DOLLS
http://wwvisions.com/craftbb/antique.html

CLOTH DOLLS
http://www.wwvisions.com/craftbb/dolls.html

COMPOSITION DOLLS
http://www.wwvisions.com/craftbb/composition.html

EXCLUSIVELY GINNY
http://www.wwvisions.com/craftbb/ginnydolls.html

HARD PLASTIC DOLL BULLETIN BOARD
http://www.wwvisions.com/craftbb/plasticdoll.html

PAPER DOLLS
http://www.wwvisions.com/craftbb/paperdoll.html

PORCELAIN DOLLS
http://www.wwvisions.com/craftbb/porcelaindolls.html

VINYL DOLLS
http://wwvisions.com/craftbb/vinyldolls.html

Surf Web Rings to Visit the Web Sites of Other Doll Collectors

A Web ring is a group of Web pages that share a similar subject and which link to each other. You travel a Web ring by clicking from one site to the next through the Web ring logo at the bottom of the pages. You don't need to join a ring in order to surf the Web pages that are part of it. Here are some popular Web rings for doll collectors.

ANTIQUE DOLL LOVERS WEB RING
http://members.aol.com/VintajBebe/ring/antiqd.html

ART DOLL WEB RING
http://members.aol.com/PretyBebe/dollart.html

TYLER DOLL WEB RING
http://auntie.com/tylerwebring.asp

MADAME ALEXANDER COLLECTORS WEB RING
http://www.cyberramp.net/~lfurlet/webring/index.htm

GENE COLLECTORS WEB RING
http://www.webring.org/cgi-bin/webring?ring=genedolls&list

SASHA DOLL WEB RING
http://members.aol.com/smplygrace/Sainfo.html

CHATTY CATHY WEB RING
http://members.aol.com/thechatrbx/index2.html

THE VINTAGE BARBIE WEB RING
http://members.aol.com/VintajBebe/barbie/ring.html

free Doll-Making Hangouts in Cyberspace

Where do doll makers hang out in cyberspace? Everywhere. You'll find them chatting on America Online, posting messages on Web sites, and exchanging tips in mailing lists. Doll makers are gregarious and love company. Tap into some of the discussion groups in this chapter and your life as a doll lover will never be the same!

🐻 Mailing List Discussion Groups for Doll Makers

Mailing lists are where the most knowledge is shared on the Internet. There are many wonderful discussion groups for doll makers. Some are for professional or aspiring doll artists, while others are for crafters who sew not only dolls but also other stuffed creatures like teddy bears. Some are serious-minded and require that participants stick to designated topics, while other groups are laid-back and encourage palaver about spouses and children. Before you sign up, read the rules of the list carefully.

We've sprinkled mailing list recommendations throughout this book. In this chapter, we've included information on how to join some of the more well-known, general-interest doll making mailing lists.

You should head to the Web page listed below to read the directions on how to join the list. In most instances, you'll need to send an e-mail message to a computer that will add you to the mailing list. It will send you a confirmation message telling you that you're signed up. After that, any messages posted to the list will arrive in your mailbox each day.

Doll Makers' Mailing Lists Are Fun and Informative, but You Need to Follow the Rules

Before you sign up for a mailing list, be sure to read its rules for posting messages to the list. Then follow our tips on mailing list netiquette.

• **When you join a mailing list, the computer that runs the list will automatically mail you directions for participating. Print them, and keep them near at hand.** Take note of the list's different e-mail addresses. You will be sending mail to one address and any subscription changes to a different "administrative" address. *Don't send messages to subscribe or unsubscribe to the list to the address that will broadcast your message to everyone!*

• **You probably have only a limited amount of disk space on your ISP to store incoming e-mail. That means that if you're a member of a mailing list that generates lots of mail, the mail may overrun your mailbox if you don't check your e-mail daily.** When that happens, e-mail that people send you will bounce back to them, and the list may automatically unsubscribe you because messages are bouncing back. The solution is to subscribe to the digest version of the list, if one is available, and unsubscribe from the list if you're going out of town.

• **Don't use free e-mail services like Juno or Hotmail to join mailing lists.** These services permit you to receive only a limited amount of e-mail, and when the list mail starts to overrun your mailbox the mailing list is going to bump you off the list. In fact, some mailing list owners will not permit subscribers with e-mail address on services like Yahoo or Hotmail.

• **If the mailing list has rules about how mail to the list should be addressed, follow them.** Many lists request that members include the list's name in the subject line of any messages so that members who have set up their e-mail software to filter messages can do so effectively. You should also try to make the subject line of your message as informative as possible for readers who don't have time to read every message posted to the list.

• **Never include your address, phone number or other personal information in a mailing list post.** Many mailing lists are archived—which means that everyone on the Internet might be able to read them until the end of time!

• **When replying to a message, take a look at the message's address to check where it's going before you hit the Send button.** Don't send a personal reply to everyone on the mailing list. And don't hit **Reply to All** if the message is addressed to many different people or lists.

Here are a few mailing list terms you might encounter:

Moderated List—All messages that are mailed to the list are first sent to a moderator, who screens them before broadcasting them to everyone on the list. It's not censorship, merely a tactic to keep messages to the topic under discussion and, on some lists, to prevent "flame wars" from breaking out between disagreeing members.

Unmoderated List—Messages are not screened.

Digest—Messages are collected into one long e-mail message that is sent to members who subscribe to the list's "digest version" at the end of the day.

Archive—Some mailing list messages are stored in vast libraries on a Web site for others to search and read years later.

FAQ—Most lists have a "frequently asked question" file that contains questions to answers that list members commonly ask. Usually the FAQ is stored on the list's Web site, although some lists allow members to retrieve the file through e-mail.

THE CLOTH DOLL CONNECTION'S MAILING LIST DIRECTORY
http://www.clothdollconnection.com/EventsandList.html#CLASSES

Karen Samuelsen maintains a wonderful, up-to-date list of discussion groups for cloth doll makers around the Internet.

HOW TO FIND A DOLL CLUB, BY JIM WINER
http://www.weaverofwebs.com/LetsTalk/Features/Features.htm

Jim, from Mimi's Everything for Doll-Making, tells you all you need to know about finding and participating in doll clubs on the Internet, including tips about nettiquette, chat rooms, and hanging out with the doll-makers on Usenet.

ANGEL OR A WILD ONE
http://www.topica.com/lists/AWO

Janet Smith runs this mailing list discussion group for cloth doll makers who fashion angels or "wild, voluptuous women."

BLACK CLOTH DOLL ART
http://www.onelist.com/subscribe.cgi/blackclothdollart

This group discusses crafting dolls with ethnic skin fabrics.

CLOTH DOLLMAKER
http://www.onelist.com/subscribe.cgi/Cloth_Dollmaker

This chat group is for doll makers, but members are encouraged to discuss "families, pets, hopes, and dreams."

CLOTHTALK
http://www.martydoll.com/ClothTalk.htm

This discussion group is for doll makers—there are over 300 on the list—but it is also for quilters, felters, dyers, weavers, and other needle artists, and the list encourages incorporation of other crafts into doll-making. Members include those new to doll-making as well as professionals.

DOLLIES DOWN UNDER DIGEST
http://members.xoom.com/dolliesunder/join.html

Two Aussie doll makers started this list, but you don't have to be from the Land of the Koala to join.

DOLLS N' SUCH SISTERHOOD

Pat Van Horn (vanhorn@servtech.com) runs this amicable list for makers of dolls, teddies, and other stuffed animals. The group hosts swaps and secret pals—and is devoted to friendliness.

DOLL STREET DREAMERS
http://www.quiltropolis.com

You'll find them in the City of Dolltropolis. Their credo is "Doll makers just want to have fun." There is sometimes a small membership fee to join.

FRIENDS OF CLOTH DOLLS
http://www.thedollnet.com/clothdolls/subscribe.html
http://www.thedollnet.com/friends

This discussion group is for anyone who loves cloth dolls, from artists to collectors and retailers. Discussions stick to the topic, but the group is lively. The group has doll making projects and hosts many activities, including swaps.

DOLLMAKERS
http://www.everink.com/dm/index.html

Dollmakers is for professional and beginning doll makers who wish to talk shop about costuming, techniques, marketing shops, magazines, shows, and so forth. Off-topic chit-chat is discouraged.

Web Bulletin Board Discussion Groups for Doll Makers

To join in these discussion groups, just head to the given URL with your Web browser. You may need to register on the Web site by providing your e-mail address and selecting a password.

DELPHI'S A GATHERING OF DOLL ARTISTS FORUM
http://www.delphi.com/artistdolls/start

A Web gathering place for artists who create "one of a kind dolls." There are bulletin boards and chat rooms for doll artists. You'll find information on shows, doll sculpting, and more.

DELPHI'S DOLL MAKING AND DOLL ARTISAN
http://www.delphi.com/Dollmaking/start

Doll Making is a discussion group for makers of porcelain and sculpted modern dolls. Doll Artisan is devoted to the reproduction of antique dolls.

DELPHI'S DE BLACK SHEEP FORUM
http://www.delphi.com/dblacksheep/start

A discussion forum for "primitive crafts," including the making of rag dolls. There's a primitive cloth doll message exchange.

More Places in Cyberspace Where Doll Makers and Lovers Hang Out

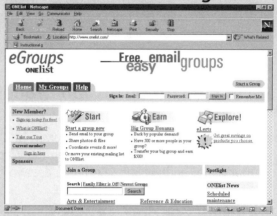

eGroups
http://www.egroups.com

You'll find dozens of groups of doll lovers chatting it up at eGroups (**http://www.egroups.com**). Most of these groups are for doll collectors, but there are some for doll makers as well. You can read messages by tapping into eGroups' Web site or by subscribing to the discussion mailing list.

In the past, in order to set up a special-interest mailing list group you needed to contact your Internet service and grapple with the puzzles of its mailing list software. An increasing number of Web sites let you set up your own mailing list or bulletin board-style discussion group for free. What's the catch? An ad might flash on your members' computer screens, but that's about it.

Many doll and teddy lovers have set up discussion groups on services such as eGroups/Onelist. To find these groups, head to the service's main Web page and type "doll" or "teddy" into the search box. In order to join the cyber-klatch, you'll need to register on the service, and may also need to e-mail the discussion moderator to ask if you can join. These services often give you the choice of reading messages bulletin-board style or having messages that other members post e-mailed directly to you.

 *What's ICQ?*

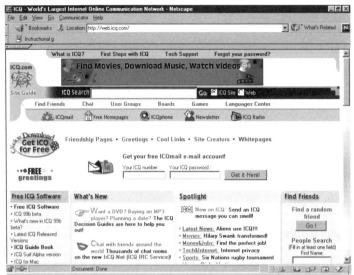

Chat with doll-making friends with ICQ, a free little program you can download from the ICQ Web site.

ICQ, named after the phrase "I Seek You," is a free chat program similar to America Online's Instant Messenger. Once you install it, whenever you tap into the Internet, it logs you into the ICQ network, informing your friends that you've come online and informing you if they're online. Many needleworkers use it to keep in touch—you often spot ICQ "call numbers" at the end of e-mail messages. You can send each other instant messages, exchange files, and chat as if you were both in an Internet chat room. It offers a number of privacy features that go beyond those in AOL's Instant Messenger. You can set ICQ to tell friends that you're online but don't wish to be disturbed, for instance. You can also set ICQ to prevent strangers from sending you unsolicited messages. You can download ICQ in both PC and Mac flavors from ICQ Inc. (**http://www.icq.com**).

Usenet Newsgroup Discussions

Newsgroups are public discussion groups that you read with your Web browser's news reader. Head to Chapter 1 for directions on how to tap in with your specific browser. In general, needlework newsgroups are less personable and chatty in tone than mailing lists. (We think they're less fun.) Nonetheless, stitchers share valuable information in them. Here are some of the newsgroups where you'll find doll lovers hanging out. We list more in Chapter 1, page 39.

rec.crafts.misc

rec.crafts.textiles.quilting

rec.crafts.textiles.needlework

rec.crafts.textiles.sewing

rec.crafts.textiles.yarn

rec.crafts.textiles.misc

rec.crafts.polymer-clay

alt.crafts. professional

bit.listserv.clayart

uk.rec.crafts

rec.collecting.dolls

rec.toys.misc

Chat With Doll Makers on America Online

Doll Makers on AOL hold weekly chats. To join them, click the **People** icon at the top of your AOL screen. Click **People Connection**, then **Find a Chat**. By moving the scroll bar in the box on the left, scroll to "Special Interest". In the box on the right, scroll to "Crafts Fabricrafts". That will get you into the Fabricrafts chat room. No one there? Click the chat schedule icon to get a weekly schedule of AOL chats. If you'd like to add the Fabricrafts chat room to your Favorites, click the Red Heart when you're in the chat room. When prompted, click **Add to Favorites**.

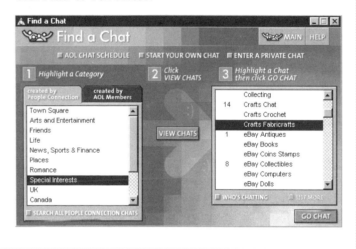

Find Web Pages of Doll Makers on America Online

Many doll makers host Web pages through America Online that offer advice, pictures, and links to other doll information on the Web. To find them if you're on AOL, use the keywords **aol hometown** and search for "doll." If you're not on AOL, head to: **http://hometown.aol.com**.

CHAPTER 5

free Help For Making Cloth Dolls

Who better to learn doll-making from than another doll maker? Many doll makers offer tutorials and snippets of advice for fashioning hands and feet, styling hair, and painting faces on their Web sites. The large doll sites that we recommend in Chapter 2 offer lots of help for stitching up dolls. You'll find links to Web sites with free doll patterns in Chapter 6. But here are some sites that offer even more good advice—and inspiration, too.

DOLL STREET FIBER LIBRARY
http://www.dollstreetdreamers.com/Liberary.htm

DOLL STREET BACK ALLEY
http://www.dollstreetdreamers.com/backalley.htm

Head to Doll Street's Web site, where you can read back issues of the Doll Street Gazette and get such indispensable tips as how to make a curling iron for dolls and how to preserve favorite doll patterns. In the Backalley, you'll find more free tutorials, including free classes on enlarging patterns and using colors.

MIMI'S HANDBOOK FOR DOLL MAKERS
http://www.mimidolls.com/handbook/handbook.htm

Gloria J. "Mimi" Winer offers this amazing resource, which offers advice on just about every subject of importance to doll makers: cleaning dolls; buying and caring for brushes; starting a doll club; face painting; using fabric; fashioning fingers, hair, and joints; needle sculpting; photographing your doll; teaching workshops; choosing doll making tools; and learning about copyright concerns.

CLOTHART TIPS AND TECHNIQUES
http://www.martydoll.com/Tips,Techniques.htm

© 2000 Marty Donnellan

Marty Donnellan offers some great techniques and advice, including instructions for hardening a needle-sculpted nylon doll (so the nylon face doesn't run) and making wigs.

DOLL-MAKING TECHNIQUES FROM CHIHARU KIKUCHI
http://www.asahi-net.or.jp/~eq5k-mgry/tech.htm

A Japanese artist offers illustrated techniques for sculpting doll faces, hands, and feet.

"HOW TO MAKE LIFE-LIKE EYES" FROM THE CLOTH DOLL ONLINE
http://www.wwvisions.com/clothdoll/eyes.html

Lisa Lichtenfels explains how even a novice doll maker can create lifelike eyes in their soft-sculpture dolls.

🛒 ANTONETTE CELY'S DOLL MAKING HELP
http://www.cely.com/doll.html

This world-renowned doll artist offers illustrated tips and tutorials on a variety of techniques, including how to properly fashion hands. Some of our favorite tutorials include:

ANTONETTE CELY'S TIPS AND TECHNIQUES FOR BETTER DOLLMAKING—WEFTING HAIR
http://www.cely.com/tips.html

© 1999 Cely Communications, Inc.

ANTONETTE CELY'S TIPS AND TECHNIQUES FOR BETTER DOLLMAKING—SEVEN TIPS TO BETTER HANDS
http://www.cely.com/dolltips.html

STUFFING TECHNIQUES
http://www.cely.com/vol2ex.html

This excerpt from Cloth Dollmaking, *by Antonette Cely, explains how you can use anything you want—dried beans, sand, sawdust, cotton batting, and so on—to stuff a doll, how to create lumps, and how not to create them.*

Take a Doll Making Class In Cyberspace

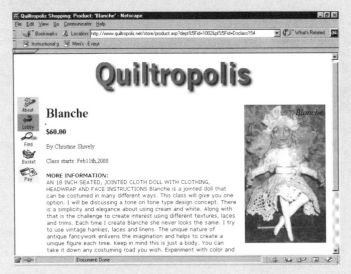

Learn how to make Blanche through an online doll-making class at Quiltropolis.

Do you live miles from a craft store that offers doll making classes? Why not take a class on the Web? A growing number of Web sites offer "classes" in cyberspace in which you can learn how to paint faces, draft doll clothing patterns, and form perfect hands. They usually cost from $25 to $60, not including supplies. Once you pay the fee you can tap into a password-protected bulletin board or Web site where you'll converse with the other class members and teachers. You'll receive an illustrated pattern and instructions. You'll need to provide your own materials, but can often buy them from the Web site or from recommended Web retailers. The Web sites on the following page offer doll making classes.

CLOTHART WORKSHOPS
http://www.martydoll.com/Workshops.htm

CRAFTY COLLEGE
http://craftycollege.com/academics/index.html

QUILTROPOLIS DOLL STREET CLASSES
http://www.quiltropolis.com

PORCELAIN DOLLMAKING CLASSES FROM PAWZ10 FOR THE DOLLMAKER
http://www.pawzfordolls.com/pawzclass.htm

CHAPTER 6

free Cloth Doll and Doll Clothing Patterns

Want to sew a frog doll? How about a cherub to sit atop a doorway? Maybe you'd like to sew a ballerina draft stopper or an Indian girl hugging her pet foxes. Tap into these Web sites for free doll patterns that will challenge your skills as well as your imagination. While you're visiting the Web site, be sure to drop a note of thanks to the pattern's designer for so generously giving of their creativity in cyberspace.

THE DOLL STREET DREAMERS' BACKALLEY
http://www.dollstreetdreamers.com/backalley.htm

At the Web home of the Doll Street Dreamers online doll club, you can get a free pattern for a full-sized doll—and a doll pin as well.

INDIAN GIRL WITH FOXES FROM ARLENE'S ORIGINAL DESIGNS
http://thedollnet.com/arlene/indian/index.html

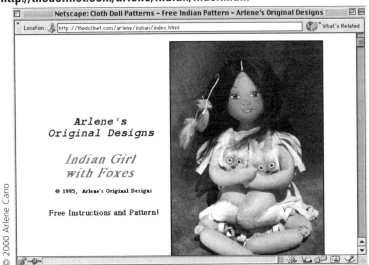

© 2000 Arlene Cano

Stitch up an adorable girl doll and her pets. While you're at Arlene's, check out her other doll patterns.

KAREN SAMUELSON'S LINKS TO DOLL PATTERNS AT THE CLOTH DOLL CONNECTION
http://www.clothdollconnection.com/FreePatterns.html

Karen offers links to free doll patterns around the Web. She keeps this directory up-to-date and tells you where to find patterns for everything from fairy doll pins to frog dolls, courtesy of doll makers around the Web.

"MEGAN" DOLL PATTERN BY KAREN CUSICK
http://www.theclothdoll.com/megan.html

Karen offers illustrated instructions for sewing a 9" jointed doll with hair and a painted face. She also offers clothing patterns.

FREE DOLL PATTERNS FROM FAIRFIELD
http://www.poly-fil.com

Fairfield Processing Corp., makers of Poly-Fil, offers a library of cloth doll patterns. Some include:

Sunny Bear
http://www.poly-fil.com/crafts/CraftProject.html

Cousin Ezra
http://www.poly-fil.com/crafts/archive/CraftProject-9903.html

My Cats: Caroline & Charley
http://www.poly-fil.com/crafts/archive/CraftProject-9801.html

My Pup: Patrick
http://www.poly-fil.com/crafts/archive/CraftProject-9802.html

Carrot Bunny
http://www.poly-fil.com/crafts/archive/CraftProject-9804.html

Earth Angel
http://www.poly-fil.com/crafts/archive/CraftProject-9806.html

Poly-Frog
http://www.poly-fil.com/crafts/archive/CraftProject-9808.html

Poly-Fil Witch
http://www.poly-fil.com/crafts/archive/CraftProject-9810.html

Ballerina Draft Stopper
http://www.poly-fil.com/crafts/archive/CraftProject-9901.html

Stylin' Stegosaurus
http://www.poly-fil.com/crafts/stegosaurus.html

CRAFTY VISIONS NEWSLETTER PATTERNS
http://wwvisions.com/newsletter

Crafty Visions offers occasional free doll patterns for things like a cupid doll and a fairy doll.

DOLL NET FREE PATTERNS
http://www.thedollnet.com

Doll Net offers a large directory of the Web sites of doll artists offering free patterns online.

SOCK BABIES BY DIANE LEWIS
http://www.wwvisions.com/newsletter/july99/sockdoll.html

Learn how to make these adorable dolls out of a pair of socks, from Crafty Visions Newsletter.

DRACO THE DRAGON PIN FROM LEE MENCONI-STEIGER
http://members.tripod.com/~wingsnthings/draco.htm

Lee offers a pattern for a dragon you can pin on your blouse.

JOINTED BALLERINA BUNNY PATTERN FROM GAIL KELLISON
http://www.netins.net/showcase/dollpatterns/Freepattern2.htm

Everyone knows that bunnies were really intended to be ballerinas. Learn how to make reality confirm to your imagination.

JUDI'S DOLLS
http://www.thedollnet.com/judi/index.html

Scroll to the bottom of the page for a free frog and a free angel pattern.

THE SWEATER GIRL FROM CASEY DOLLS
http://www.caseydolls.com/sweater.html

Doll maker Jacqueline Casey offers directions for making a terrific doll out of the back of an old sweater. This is one artsy-looking doll!

CHERUB PATTERN FROM GAIL'S STITCH N' SPLINTER PATTERNS

http://www.thedollnet.com/stitchnsplinter/index.html

Gail sells doll patterns, but she also offers freebies.

ANGEL PATTERN FROM SISTERS & DAUGHTERS
http://www.sistersanddaughters.com/angel/index.html

Sisters & Daughters sells patterns and supplies, but also offers freebies, including the pattern for Angela, a tree topper angel.

HOW TO MAKE AN <EXPLETIVE DELETED> DOLL
http://www.huskins.com/strega/dammit.html

Do you sometimes fantasize about being seven years old again and whacking your doll against the wall in frustration? Weezie's Warped World offers a pattern for a doll that you can beat the stuffing out of without feeling any remorse. She also offers an accompanying poem.

🛒 BABY PATTERN FROM STITCH 'N STUFF
http://www.snsdolls.com/fpattern/8inchbaby/babymain.htm

Instructions for this adorable doll come courtesy of Cloth Dolls by Stitch 'N Stuff.

CRAFTER'S DIRECTORY DOLL PROJECTS
http://crafterscommunity.com/members/links/Projects/Dolls

You'll find links to doll patterns around the Web, including an adorable jointed cherub.

EMILY DOLL FROM CRAFTER'S COMMUNITY
http://crafterscommunity.com/projects/sewing/emily.html

Learn how Emily came to life and how you can make this lovely doll.

A CHARMING SHELF BUNNY FROM CRAFTER'S COMMUNITY
http://crafterscommunity.com/projects/sewing/bunny.html

Instructions for making a lovely soft-sculpture bunny.

🛒 ANGEL PLASTIC BAG HOLDER FROM STITCH 'N STUFF
http://www.snsdolls.com/fpattern/angelbag/bagmain.htm

Make a 29-inch angel to hold your bags.

🛒 "MILLI" BY UTE VASINA
http://enchantingdelights.com/free.htm

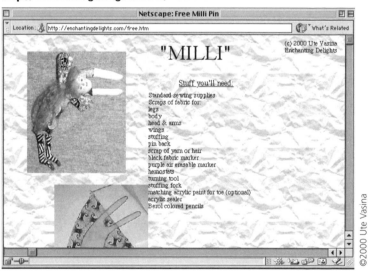

Ute Vasina designed and shares directions for this charming doll pin.

SMALLWORKS — CLOTH HAND DOLL PATTERN
http://www.smallwork.com/page/hands.html

Melinda Small Paterson shares a free pattern for hands with different meanings, including "I love you" in American Sign Language.

HANDWORK LESSON FROM CHIHARU KIKUCHI
http://www.asahi-net.or.jp/%7Eeq5k-mgry/handwork_e.htm

Chiharu provides the pattern and instructions for Wizard of Oz dolls, a sumo wrestler doll (inspired by a teddy bear!), and a small mascot doll.

BOO-BOO BUNNY BY VICTORIA WHITE
http://getcreativeshow.com/Crafting_Sewing_Conference_Center/
craft_sewing_seminars/boo_boo_bunny.htm

Learn how to make this charming bunny. The bunny's back has a place to hold an ice cube, making it great for soothing little cuts or scraps.

Free Doll Clothes Patterns

PATTI'S QUICK & EASY SHOE FOR ANY DOLL
http://www.PMCDesigns.com/shoepattern.htm

Doll maker Patti Medaris offers illustrated directions for making doll shoes.

🛒 DOLL SHOE PATTERN FROM STITCH 'N STUFF
http://www.snsdolls.com/fpattern/dollshoe/shoemain.htm

This site provides patterns for making shoes that will fit most 18" vinyl dolls. The directions show how to adjust the pattern for dolls of other sizes.

DRESS A LITTLE COUNTRY GIRL IN A COTTON DRESS AND PINAFORE BY JOY PARKER
http://www.csolve.net/~minidoll/countrygirl.htm

CUSTOM DOLLS
http://www.customdolls.com

Custom Dolls offers a collection of wonderful sewing how-tos and related articles for doll makers. Here are some of our favorites:

Simple Sewing for Simple Fashions by Dolla Butler
http://www.employees.org/~jbp/customdolls/seweasy/dress.html

Kimono for Barbie-Sized Dolls by Holly Ingraham
http://www.employees.org/~jbp/customdolls/kimono/kimono.html

Instructions for Putting in a Tiny Zipper by Lisa Barger
http://www.employees.org/~jbp/customdolls/tinyzippers/
zippage1.html

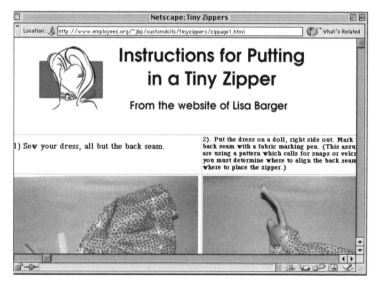

Be sure to visit the January 2000 issue
(**http://members.theglobe.com/customdoll/decjanfeb/index.html**),
which includes "Jewelry Making for the Fashion Doll" and "How to Paint Shoes."

"HOW TO MAKE YOUR OWN DOLL BUTTONS" BY LEE MENCONI-STEIGER
http://members.tripod.com/~wingsnthings/button.htm

Lee offers directions for making your own attractive buttons from clay and other elements.

"USING PERIOD FASHION PATTERN BOOKS TO MAKE DOLL COSTUMES" BY MARY B. LYTLE
http://home.flash.net/~liebling/per_fash_patterns.htm
Learn a simple procedure for making custom doll clothes from those wonderful patterns in historical costume design textbooks.

For ideas about sewing historical costumes for your dolls, head to **The Costume Gallery** (**http://www.costumegallery.com**). It offers over 1,800 pictures of historical clothing. At **The Victoriana Study Center, Harpers Bazaar Magazine** (**http://www.victoriana.com/library/harpers/harpers.html**) you can read fashion magazine articles from the 19th-century. **The Elizabethan Costuming Page** (**http://www.dnaco.net/~aleed/corsets**) will fill you in on dress in the age of Shakespeare.

Bedazzle Your Doll's Clothing With Beads and Fancy Stitches To learn about the art of beading, head to BeadNet (**http://www.mcs.net/~simone/beadnet.html**). You'll find lots of free beading instructions, projects, and patterns. To learn how to fashion delicate silk blossoms and leaves on garments, head to the **Silk Ribbon Embroidery Stitch Dictionary** (**http://www.ribbonworks.com/stitch/stitch.html**). For general embroidery instruction and stitch guides, head to **Sharon Boggon's Needlework Stitch Dictionary** (**http://www.anu.edu.au/ITA/CSA/textiles/sharonb/stitches/stitchfsite.html**).

CHAPTER 7

free Help for Making Porcelain And Clay Dolls

Porcelain dolls are beautiful, with their finely painted faces and delicate hands. But could you really make one? Why not? You'll find illustrated tutorials on molding porcelain dolls on many of the Web sites devoted to the craft. You'll also find instructions on sculpting dolls from clay and resins on many of the sites we recommend in this chapter. But the best way to learn how to create porcelain or clay dolls is by taking a class. Some of the Web sites devoted to making porcelain dolls offer "cyber-classes"—you pay a fee, buy the materials through the Web site, then obtain online instructions through Web pages (and maybe a discussion group or video as well).

To learn about doll-making classes in your area, visit Web site of the **International Foundation of Doll Makers** (**http://ifdm.org**).

 *Free How-Tos for Getting Starting Making Porcelain or Clay Dolls*

SO YOU WANT TO BE A DOLL MAKER! PORCELAIN REPRODUCTION DOLL MAKING
http://collectdolls.about.com/hobbies/collectdolls/ library/weekly/aa110999.htm

HOW TO POUR A PORCELAIN DOLL HEAD MOLD
http://collectdolls.about.com/hobbies/collectdolls/ library/howto/ht1.htm

A nice introduction to the art of creating porcelain dolls from Denise Van Patten at About.Com.

A SCULPTING DEMONSTRATION OVERVIEW BY BLUFROGG GARDENS
http://www.blufrogg.com/dolls/sculpt_demo.htm

BluFrogg Gardens offers a well-illustrated tutorial on sculpting doll faces from clay. The Web site offers a wonderful bulletin board where doll artists can discuss sculpting. On the distance learning page (**http://www.blufrogg.com/dolls/distance_learning.htm**), you can sign up for a long-distance course for $25 which includes four lessons, a CD with video instruction, and access to private Web pages.

MAKING A PUPPET HEAD
http://members.efortress.com/temtool/heads.html

Dan Butterworth shows how he molds puppet heads.

🛒 ONLINE MOLD MAKING CLASSES
http://www.lindakays.com/molds.htm

Linda J. Kays demonstrates how to reproduce a cold cast resin sculpture.

SCULPTING A HEAD DIRECTLY INTO PORCELAIN WITHOUT MOLDS
http://home.wxs.nl/~marlaine/sculptm.htm

Doll artist Marlaine Verhelst explains that ceramists have sculpted dolls from porcelain for centuries and describes how to do it yourself.

HOW TO MAKE YOUR OWN DOLLS
http://people.zeelandnet.nl/mgstaa/webdoc3e.htm

Mary Staa and Ria Jacobi demonstrate through pictures the steps involved in fashioning dolls from clay.

HOW TO MAKE NOAH'S DOLL
http://www2d.biglobe.ne.jp/~dhnoah/make_00.htm

Here is a good tutorial on how to assemble a ball-jointed doll. In other words, you use ball-and-socket joints in the doll's body, arms, and legs, and the doll's limbs and head are joined together by loops of elastic. This site includes complete illustrated directions for making such a doll using sawdust and stone clay.

PAPIER MACHE REDISCOVERED BY RONNIE BURKETT
http://www.arvotek.net/~props/papier.html

Renowned Canadian puppeteer Ronnie Burkett tells you all you need to know to use paper maché in your next doll project. He offers his five favorite recipes for paper maché pulp. Each uses some variation of paper, adhesive, and filler. He explains how you can experiment with paper maché recipes—adding more adhesive for a stronger finish, for example—to create the perfect mix for your project.

Polymer Clay Shoppe offers a large directory of the Web sites of doll artists who use polymer clay (**http://polymerclayshoppe.com/polyclaydoll.htm**). Visit these sites for inspiration and fun—and advice, too!

 *More Free How-Tos on Molding Dolls*

🛒 WHAT IS SLIP CASTING FROM RYKER STUDIOS
http://www.rykerstudios.com/articles/slipcasting.htm

Learn about slip and slip casting and how to open a mold.

PROCEDURE FOR MAKING SILICONE MOLDS
http://www.cs.cmu.edu/~rapidproto/manufacturing/
molds/silicone.html

This site from Carnegie Mellon University explains how to make silicone molds.

LACE DRAPED DOLLS FROM PORCELAIN MAKERS INTERNATIONAL ONLINE
http://www.porcelainpainters.com/lacedoll.htm

On this site, you'll learn how to make gorgeous lace draped dolls from Bonnie Crandall, also known as "Nebraskalassie."

ALUMILITE'S HOW TO GUIDE OF MOLD MAKING
http://www.alumilite.com/alumilitemoldmaking.htm

Alumilite is a two-part liquid plastic casting resin. This site includes a step-by-step mold-making guide and information on how this product can be used to makes duplicates of original dolls.

POR-A-KAST MOLD MAKING AND CASTING SYSTEMS
http://www.synair.com/products/pak/index.html
http://www.synair.com/products/pam/pam_howtoindex.html

Por-A-Kast is a liquid urethane resin casting material in a spreadable paste form. This site includes an explanation of urethanes and mold making instructions.

Visit **Sculptor.Org** (**http://www.Sculptor.Org**) from Richard Collins for links to sculpting help around the Web, including advise on materials, research, associations, tools, technology, tips, and more.

🧸 *More Free Tips for Making Porcelain and Clay Dolls*

TIPS AND TRICKS FOR PORCELAIN DOLL-MAKING FROM DENIS VAN PATTEN DOLLS
http://www.dollymaker.com/tipsand.htm

Tips on kiln firing, porcelain painting, greenware, pouring molds, and stringing.

🛒 DOLL-MAKING TIPS FROM MARGOS PORCELAIN DOLLS AND DOLL SUPPLIES
http://www.margosdolls.com/tips.htm

To prevent air bubbles, strain your slip twice before using. Read tips from professional doll makers and other visitors to the site.

DOLL-MAKING TIPS FROM THE ORIGINAL DOLL ARTIST COUNCIL OF AMERICA
http://www.odaca.org/dollmak.htm

Member artists of the ODACA share tips on crafting porcelain and clay dolls. You'll learn how to condition polymer clay, make teeth for a sculpted doll, avoid discolorations in polymer clay, and more.

🛒 HELPFUL TIPS FROM MINIWORLD
http://www.miniworlddolls.com/HT_Home.htm

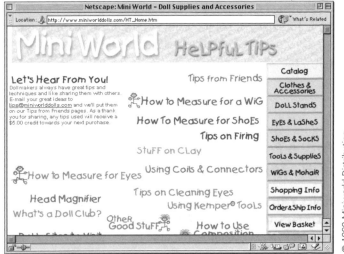

This page offers a guide to the doll-making tips found throughout the MiniWorld Web site. You'll find advice on how to fire doll heads, use coils and connectors, measure for wigs, and work with and measure for eyes.

 If you can't find porcelain doll-making supplies in your town, check out these Web retailers:

BELL CERAMICS
http://www.bellceramics.com
CLASSIC DOLLS
http://www.classicdolls.com
MINIATURE PORCELAIN DOLL ARTISTRY
http://www.minidolls.com
BASS RIVER DOLL WORKS
http://www.bassriverdollworks.com
G.E.M. DOLL EMPORIUM
http://www.gemdoll.com
ALL FOR A DOLL
http://www.allforadoll.com.

Discussion Groups for Porcelain and Clay Doll Makers

The best way to learn about how to create dolls from porcelain and clay is to talk about it with other doll makers. Tap into these discussion groups for fun and advice.

POLYMER CLAY CENTRAL AT DELPHI
http://www.delphi.com/polymerclay/start

Tap into this cyber-meeting place for fans of polymer clay. Share tips, and swap projects and info. You need to register with Delphi to tap in, but it's free.

DOLL MAKERS FORUM
http://www.wwvisions.com/craftbb/porcelaindolls.html

This is a busy discussion group for porcelain doll makers.

PORCELAIN DOLL EGROUPS MAILING LIST
http://www.eGroups.com/list/porcelaindolls

THE PORCELAIN DOLL-MAKING MAILING LIST
http://www.egroups.com/list/dollmaking/info.html

To join in this doll makers' discussion group, send an empty e-mail to dollmaking-subscribe@makelist.com, or head to the above Web page.

DELPHI'S DOLL-MAKING AND DOLL ARTISAN
http://www.delphi.com/Dollmaking/start

Doll Making is a discussion group for makers of porcelain and sculpted modern dolls. Doll Artisan is devoted to the reproduction of antique dolls.

free Help Caring for and Restoring Dolls

We all have one tucked in a closet—a battered doll that, in a previous life now hard to remember, fell off the back of a tricycle one too many times. Because we still love that old doll and the innocent days she evokes, we often buy similarly love-worn dolls at fleamarkets or garage sales. Fixing a broken doll is a lot like fixing a broken soul. You never know what kind of smile will emerge when you wipe the grime of years off a face. You never know what color of hair will shine forth when you snip off a torn bonnet. In this chapter, we've listed Web sites that offer advice on restoring and caring for dolls. There are lots of doll hospitals on the Web too—we can't lead you to them all, but many of the Web sites in this chapter will. We've also included a directory of Web sites that offer advice on caring for antique ceramics, lace, and other textiles at the end of this chapter. We've even listed Web sites that offer doll history lessons.

"FIXING UP SHIRLEY TEMPLE COMPOSITION DOLLS"
http://members.aol.com/JAB105/shirley/shirlfix.html

"KEEPING YOUR SHIRLEY TEMPLE COMPOSITION DOLLS BEAUTIFUL"
http://members.aol.com/JAB105/shirley/humid.html

Good advice for taking care of all composition dolls, from a Shirley Temple collector.

DOLL REPAIR AT SUITE 101
http://www.suite101.com/welcome.cfm/doll_repair

Melissa Beck offers features on repairing dolls, plus links to many doll repair resources around the Web. You'll read about rerooting hair and why people buy broken dolls to repair.

MADAME ALEXANDER DOLL CLUB—CLEANING DOLLS
http://www.madc.org/c1.html

You'll find advice on cleaning compo, hard plastic, vinyl, and stuffed latex dolls. There is also information on redoing hair, cleaning and repairing clothes, and repairing paint and eyelashes.

 ## DOLL RESTORATION ADVICE AT ABOUT.COM
http://collectdolls.about.com/hobbies/
collectdolls/msub30.htm

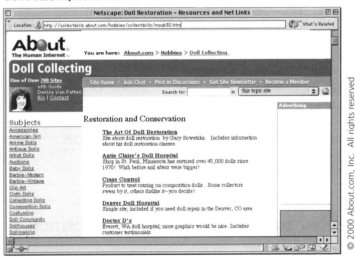

*Denise Van Patten tells you all about how to preserve dolls, care for antique dolls, display dolls and more in About.Com's doll collector's forum (**http://collectdolls.about.com**).*

CUSTOMIZING BARBIE®
http://www.employees.org/~jbp/customizing/customizing.html

Give your doll a braided hairdo and reroot her eyelashes.

VICKY'S HELPFUL TIPS
http://www.vicky-web.com/tips/main.html

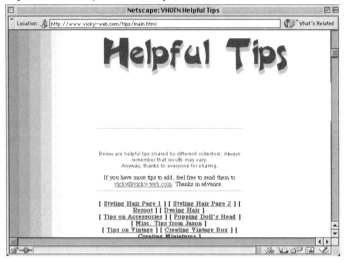

This is a large collection of tips from many different doll collectors. You'll find advice on styling hair, rerooting and dyeing hair, curing "green ear," removing tags, cleaning, and more.

CARING FOR DOLLS & TOYS
http://www.si.edu/organiza/centers/cal/dolls.html

A collection of references where one can head for advice on the care and repair of dolls and other toys, including names, addresses, phone numbers of doll museums, clubs and conservation societies.

THE PRESERVATION, STORAGE AND DISPLAY OF PRECIOUS PAPER DOLLS
http://www.opdag.com/Preserving.html

Judy M. Johnson tells you how to take care of paper dolls and keep them looking youthful.

THE ARTISTS' OWN TIPS ON REROOTING, REPAINTING, AND CUSTOMIZING YOUR DOLLS FROM DOLLRAVES
http://www.dollraves.com/arttips.html

Read two illustrated articles on rerooting, dyeing and styling hair.

TIPS ON REPAIRING AND RESTORING DOLLIKINS
http://home.att.net/~dollikin/hints.html

Dollikin collectors share their tips on repairing and restoring. Some of the hard-to-find information on this site includes advice on tightening wrist joints and using acrylic sculpting products to repair a crack or chip. There's also doll displaying advice.

WASH, SET, AND STYLE SASHA® DOLL HAIR
http://homepage.fcgnetworks.net/cstgelais/hairdo.htm

Cecile St. Gelais details how to wash Sasha® Doll's hair and how to create various hairdos, including the Shirley, pageboy, and others. The advice is applicable to other dolls.

THE BARBIE® MEDICINE CABINET
http://www.dollpage.com/html/barbie_medicine_cabinet.htm

No-Color Mascara does for Barbie® what Dippity Do does for us (well...sort of). The folks at Dollpage.Com share their favorite tricks.

HINTS AND TIPS FROM THE DOLL MALL
http://www.thedollmall.com/hints.html

There are lots of helpful articles on this site. Some subjects include exploring the world of cleaners, protecting dolls against fading, keeping pests from your dolls, taking your dolls out of storage, and insuring your dolls.

DOLL REPAIR Q&A BY GARY SOWATZKA
http://www.sowatzka.com/gary/repairqa.htm

Gary shares his extensive doll repair knowledge by answering your questions on doll repair. Leave a question for Gary or read answers to others' questions.

SELF-HELP CARE FOR SASHA® DOLLS
http://www.sashadoll.com
http://members.aol.com/SLewis11217/help.html

Susanna Lewis, museum-trained in general conservation and restoration techniques, shares advice on cleaning dolls, cleaning clothes, hair care, display, storage, and more.

Thinking Of Getting Your Dolls Appraised? Head to The Doll Appraiser (**http://www.dollappraiser.com**), run by Sharon Philbin, a member of the United Federation of Doll Clubs. You'll find appraisal information on antique, modern, and composition dolls. The site also explains doll terminology. Another helpful site is **Appraisal Related Services from Gary Sowatzka** (**http://www.sowatzka.com/gary/appraisals.htm**).

Judy often buys old and ablated dolls on the Web auction site **eBay** (**http://www.ebay.com**) and fixes them up. eBay is a great place to look for a copy of that doll that you lost while visiting your grandma when you were age seven—because you'll probably find it! Head to Chapter 13 for our tips on eBay bargain hunting.

Web Sites with General Antique Restoration Advice

ANTIQUERESTORERS.COM
http://antiquerestorers.com

On this huge Web site, you'll find articles on restoring and caring for just about anything that's old, from textiles to wooden toys.

ANTIQUES FROM THE BBC ONLINE
http://www.bbc.co.uk/antiques

"CLEANING STAINED LINEN"
http://www.bbc.co.uk/antiques/tricks/linen_stain.shtml

MRS. BIDDINGTON: DOLL HAIR RESTORATION & CARE
http://www.biddingtons.com/content/mrsdollhair.html

MRS. BIDDINGTON: LACE RESTORATION
http://www.biddingtons.com/content/mrslace.html

"AT HOME WITH LOVELY LINENS" BY PAMELA WIGGINS
http://antiques.about.com/hobbies/antiques/library/weekly/mcurrent.htm

AMERICAN INSTITUTE FOR CONSERVATION OF HISTORIC & ARTISTIC WORKS
http://palimpsest.stanford.edu/aic

Web Sites Where You Can Learn About the History of Dolls

NATIONAL GALLERY OF ART — DOLLS FROM THE INDEX OF AMERICAN DESIGN
http://www.nga.gov/collection/gallery/iaddoll/iaddoll-main1.html

Visit a beautiful Web gallery of dolls revered by collectors and displayed in galleries around the country. Each picture of a doll is accompanied by historical information.

"A BRIEF HISTORY OF ANTIQUE DOLLS" BY DENIS VAN PATTEN AT ABOUT.COM
http://collectdolls.about.com/library/weekly/
aa032799.htm?pid=2740&cob=home

Also accessible at **http://collectdolls.about.com**.

EBAY UK'S "DOLLS AND FIGURES, BRIEF HISTORY OF DOLLS"
http://www.ebay.co.uk/community/library/
catindex-dolls-history.html

On this site, you learn about the history of dolls and how to display and care for your own dolls.

DECADES OF DOLLS FROM KAYLEE'S KORNER OF COLLECTIBLE DOLLS
http://www.dollinfo.com/balloons.htm

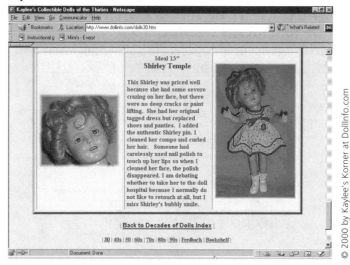

Kaylee provides a thorough decade-by-decade tour of dolls from the '30s through the '90s on her Web site. She displays pictures of cherished ones from her collection, and tells you a little about their history and why they are (or are not) valuable. This is an very educational site!

"THE HISTORY OF PAPER DOLLS" BY JUDY M. JOHNSON
http://www.opdag.com/History.html

Did you know that the first manufactured paper doll was Little Fanny, produced by S&J Fuller in London in 1810? Judy M. Johnson details a fascinating history.

BARBIE® HISTORY
http://www.barbie.com/history/history_main/history_main.asp

*At Mattel's official Barbie site (**http://www.barbie.com**) you'll get a year-by-year history of everyone's favorite doll and Barbie trivia.*

DOLLS THROUGH HISTORY FROM MARIE-CLAUDE DUPONT
http://www.cam.org/~delisle/dollasart.htm

CHAPTER 9

free Big Web Sites for Teddy Bear Makers

Teddy bear lovers are everywhere on the Web—and it's a good thing! Gone are the days when one needed to stake out mall gift shops in order to befriend other teddy fanatics. The Web sites in this chapter offer advice on collecting bears, as well as fixing and making them. Most of the Web sites also offer discussion boards where one can chat with other teddy fans. You'll also find teddy artists and collectors hanging out in many of the discussion groups for doll makers that we recommend in Chapter 4.

 🛒 **TEDDY BEARS ON THE NET**
http://www.tbonnet.com

If you're a bear lover, your first stop should be Terry Bauman's Web site for all things teddy. You'll find information on teddy discussion groups, magazines, books, shows, and more. You can buy teddy bears, read teddy design hints, and have a teddy tell your fortune.

 **BEARWORLD!**

http://www.bearworld.com

BearWorld! offers the biggest selection of teddy bear links on the Net. You'll find advice on adding joints, selecting furs, and attaching eyes. You'll also find a directory of artists who sell custom-made bears on the Web—sites that are great for inspiration.

 TEDDY BEAR DISCUSSION GROUPS AT ONELIST

http://www.onelist.com

Several teddy bear discussion groups for makers and collectors of bears are run out of the OneList service. They change frequently. To find them, head to OneList's main page and use the search feature to search for "teddy."

 COLLECTIBLES AT ABOUT.COM
http://collectibles.about.com

You'll find articles and information for bear collectors at Barbara Crews' Collectibles forum at About.Com.

THE TEDDY RUXPIN UNOFFICIAL FAQ AND MESSAGE BOARD
http://www.mindspring.com/~mathue/faq.html

Get all your questions on Teddy Ruxpin answered, including ones about repairing him.

THE TEDDY BEAR TIMES
http://www.teddybeartimes.com

Tap into the Web site of this British magazine for lovers and makers of teddy bears. There's a bulletin board where you can chat with other teddy fans around the world.

TOY COLLECTING AT ABOUT.COM
http://toycollecting.about.com

Scroll down the main page and click on Bears. At Gianfranco Origliato's Toy Collecting forum you'll find more articles on bear hoarding.

__Help for Travelling Teddy Lovers__ Planning a trip? Tap into the **Teddy Bear Store Directory** (**http://www.bearsbythesea.com/dir/storedir/index.html**) to find teddy lovers stores around the world. This directory comes courtesy of Pacific Leisure Marketing, with support from Bears by the Sea. To find the teddy stores without walking all over town, head to **Mapblast** (**http://www.mapblast.com**). Type the store's address and Mapblast will blast a map your way.

 More Big Teddy Bear Lovers' Web Sites

 TEDDY BEAR COLLECTING AT SUITE 101
http://www.suite101.com/welcome.cfm/teddy_bear_collecting

Judy Bogdan is your host for articles, discussions, and related links to Web resources for collectors.

TEDDY BEAR U.K.
http://www.teddy-bear-uk.com

This Web site for British bear lovers includes a guide to British teddy museums, artists, clubs, and suppliers. There's also bear history information, collecting tips, and "Teddy Tales."

BEARS AND BEYOND
http://www.bearsandbeyond.com

This Canadian site includes a gallery of Canadian bear artists, an events calendar, free e-mail bear postcards, and more.

THE TEDDY BEAR TIMES
http://www.niagara.com/~tbt/abttbt.html

Learn about this club for bear collectors, artists, and enthusiasts. You can read a free issue of their newsletter.

 🛒 **TEDDY BEARS DEN**

http://www.teddybearsden.com

Get plenty of teddy-making information, free e-mail teddy post cards, a bulletin board, teddy screensavers, and more.

THE BEAR MUSEUM IN PETERSFIELD

http://www.bearmuseum.co.uk

Visit the Web site of the Bear Museum located in the town of Petersfield in Hampshire, England. There's a history of bears, plus help on identifying your bear.

WHOLE POP MAGAZINE ONLINE: THE TEDDY BEAR
http://www.wholepop.com/features/teddy/index.html

The Whole Pop Magazine, an eclectic Web-based magazine with articles on popular culture, clues you in to the history of Smokey the Bear and other teddy facts and lore.

THE TEDDY BEAR GALLERY
http://www.teddybeargallery.com/index.html

You can view the work of a number of teddy artists at this showcase site.

THE GREAT TEDDY BEAR HUG
http://www.teddybears.com

Kelly Brown Brehm maintains this huge directory of teddy information, including a guide to retailers, retailers, museums, clubs, shows, artists, and more.

TEDDY BEAR MUSEUM OF NAPLES
http://www.teddybeargiftshop.com/TBGS

Take a the virtual tour of the store. There are bears, both to buy and just to ogle.

BEARS & BEDTIME MFG., INC.
http://www.bearsandbedtime.com

You'll find teddy bear-making supplies and tools, the Bear News (an online newspaper), information on Canadian bear shows, and more.

BEAR ARTISTS ONLINE
http://bearartists.com

Lisa Vollrath runs this gathering place for bear artisans. There's a bulletin board, interviews with the bear award-of-excellence winners, and more.

THE POOH WEB DIRECTORY
http://hey.to/pooh-bear

Winnie fans will adore this site. There are message boards, free electronic greeting cards, links to Pooh Web rings, and features on the history of Pooh.

Tap into the **Teddy Bear Search Engine** (**http://www.teddybearsearch.com**) to find even more Web sites devoted to bears. You can search the site in both English and French.

Web Sites of Teddy Bear Makers

Tap into the Web site of your favorite teddy manufacturer for news, bear care advice, and teddy bear fun.

STEIFF
http://www.steiff.com
http://www.steiffusa.com

The makers of the plush bears with the button in the ear (bet you had one of those as a kid!) offer bear news and information on collectors clubs on their Web site.

GUND
http://www.gund.com

HERMANN
http://www.hermann.de

RUSS BERRIE & COMPANY
http://www.russ-berrie.com

MAINE BEAR COMPANY
http://www.mainebear.com

NORTH AMERICAN BEAR COMPANY
http://www.muffy.com

HERMANN TEDDY ORIGINALS
http://hermannteddy.com
http://www.hermann.de/frmain_e.htm

*Tap into the Teddy Bear Manufacturers Directory (**http://www.teddybears.com/history/index.htm**) for a guide to teddy makers, courtesy of The Great Teddy Bear Hug.*

▮ Travel Teddy Bear Web Rings to Find More Teddies on the Net

A Web ring is a group of linked Web sites. To surf a ring you don't need to "join" it, just to click on its logo. Here are some of our favorites:

RING OF TEDDY BEARS
http://www.bearartists.com/rotb

Visit the Web sites of fellow teddy lovers by surfing the Teddy Ring.

BEAR ARTISTS ONLINE
http://bearartists.com

COLLECTIBLE TEDDY BEARS RETAILER WEBRING
http://www.thebeanpatch.com/webring/teddyBearRing.htm

Travel this ring if you're looking for Web sites of bear retailers.

BRITISH BEARS ON THE NET WEBRING
http://www.hyperchat.co.uk/u/britbears

RING OF MINI BEARS
http://users.bart.nl/~cjmdbr/ring.htm

Do You Ever Get the Feeling There Are Things You Don't Know About Your Bear? Visit "How to ID Your Bear" from Teddy Bear U.K. (**http://www.teddy-bear-uk.com/lerfram7.htm**) for advice on identifying your brand of bear. Does your bear have a label or signs of a label? Is he stuffed? This informative Web site will tell you where to head with these clues. A handy, printable Bear Profile sheet is included.

C H A P T E R   10

free Discussions for Teddy Bear Makers and Lovers

What's more fun than spending an evening hanging out with other teddy bear fans? Only another teddy bear lover can honestly tell you whether a mohair bear looks best in an argyle sweater or silk spats. Ask for such an opinion from someone who is not a teddy fanatic and they may give you that blank stare that means, "You're crazy, aren't you?" Sometimes you need a place where you can talk about teddies and nothing else. Tap into the discussion groups in this chapter for news about teddy bear collecting, help sewing teddy bears, and other teddy-related fun.

 TEDDY BEARS MAILING LIST
http://www.cybear.austin.com

This group talks about just about everything relating to teddy bears, including collecting them, crafting them, restoring them, and enjoying them.

 DOLL NET'S TEDDY BEAR BULLETIN BOARD
http://www.wwvisions.com/craftbb/teddy.html

Doll Net offers a bulletin board where bear makers can discuss their craft. There's also a lot of discussion pertaining to collecting and selling bears.

 BEARWORLD CHAT ROOMS & BULLETIN BOARD
http://www.bearworld.com

They call themselves the biggest online community of bear lovers on the Net. You'll find a bulletin board and chat rooms for bear lovers as well. This is a gathering place for both bear lovers and makers.

 **BEAR ARTISTS ONLINE**
http://bearartists.com

*In order to join this group, you must be a commercial bear artist
with a Web site where you sell your bears. You need to fill out an
application, and the requirements to join are strict. Members link
to each other via a Web ring and enjoy an ICQ user's group,
which is a chat room using the special ICQ (**http://web.icq.com**)
chat software.*

 TEDDY BEARS BULLETIN BOARD
http://www.wwvisions.com/craftbb/teddy.html

Matt Wright runs this board for teddy makers and lovers.

 BEARS AND BEYOND DISCUSSION BOARD
http://www.bearsandbeyond.com/discus/board.html

*Tap into this Canadian bear lovers message site for discussions on
topics such as "New Bears, New Hugs" and "Bear Web Site
Design."*

 ***Yet Another Place to Discuss Teddy Love***
Tap into the Usenet newsgroup
alt.collecting.teddybears to discuss your passion
with other collectors. Head to Chapter 1 for directions on how to tap into Usenet groups.

free Teddy Bear Patterns

One would think that stitching up a teddy bear would be a simple matter, and that all teddy bear patterns would be alike. Not so. Every teddy pattern helps you create a bear with a different personality, from the shape of its paws to the slant of its muzzle. Hardcore teddy bear makers know this. Fanatical teddy bear makers like to have as many bear patterns on hand as possible. Tap into the Web sites in this chapter for free bear patterns that you can print or download, as well as patterns for clothes and accessories.

Free Teddy Bear Patterns

 ### THE TEDDY BEAR TIMES PATTERN ARCHIVE
http://www.teddybeartimes.com/patterns/listing.htm

This British magazine for lovers and makers of teddy bears offers free downloadable patterns for bears, clothes, and accessories. They also offer information on suppliers and a teddy bear chat.

 BEARLY HEAVEN
http://bluebonnetvillage.com/bheaven.htm

Cynthia Farrabee, a well-known bear maker, offers a gallery of her work which will give you many ideas. She includes a free pattern.

LAURENCE VERON'S FREE TEDDY BEAR PATTERN
http://www.teddybearsearch.com/patterns

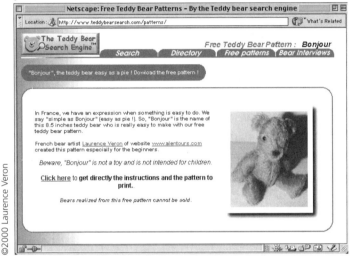

*French bear artist Veron (**http://www.alentours.com**) offers a free pattern for Bonjour, an easy-to-make 8-inch teddy*

A CROCHETED TEDDY BEAR PATTERN
http://crochet.about.com/hobbies/crochet/library/weekly/aa110897.
htm

Sandi Marshall offers a pattern for a crocheted teddy. You'll also find links to patterns for a crocheted sundress (something every she-bear needs) and a pilgrim outfit—another de rigour bear accessory.

KNITTING TEDDY BEARS
http://www.knitting-crochet.com/bearpattern.html

Jean from the Yarn Lover's Room shares instructions for knitting bears.

BASIL & BETH FROM HOW TO BUY TEDDY BEAR-MAKING SUPPLIES
http://www.ehow.com/eHow/eHow/0,1053,10429,00.html

Click "Teddy Bear Pattern Online" for a free pattern to use for making 11-inch jointed, antique-style bears. The pattern is by Gailyn of The Bear Paw Clan.

8" JOINTED BEAR BY JULIE WEGELIN
http://getcreativeshow.com/Crafting_Sewing_Conference_Center/craft_sewing_seminars/teddybear.htm

CROCHETED BEAR FINGER PUPPET
http://members.aol.com/SAG55/bear.html

Remember how you loved these as a kid? Now you can make some for little friends.

BEAR IN BUNNY'S CLOTHES
http://members.aol.com/sag55/bbunny.html

BASIC TEDDY BEAR BEAD PATTERNS BY EVELYN MC DERMAND
http://home.att.net/~mcdermand/beadies/basic.htm

free Teddy Bear-Making Tips and How-Tos

The best teddies look well-loved, with an earthy sweetness about them. Achieving those effects and giving your teddy real personality is an art like no other. The Web sites in this chapter offer some of the most wonderful collections of bear-making tips you'll read anywhere. For instance, the **Labours of Love** Web site (**http://www.laboursoflove.com**) advises that if you wish your bear to look like an old fellow, stuff him so that he slouches. The site also tells you how to dip your bear into a tea bath for an aged look, and recommends rubbing blackened fire wood on paws, ears, and nose for a well-handled look. Here are more Web sites with tips for giving your teddy personality.

🛒 BEAR MAKING TIPS FROM LABOURS OF LOVE
http://www.laboursoflove.com/p1293.htm

"Don't worry, everyone stitches the nose several times before getting it right." "When choosing your fur, remember shorter fur on smaller bears and longer fur on bigger bears." These are the sorts of tips you'll find in this compendium of bear crafting tips.

🛒 SPARE BEAR PARTS
http://www.SpareBear.com

This retailer of bear making goodies offers a huge database of bear making tips and how-tos on almost everything: joint installation, furs, repairs, how to make a new bear look old and vice versa, needle sculpting, installing music box keys. They also offer a free newsletter.

"HOW TO BUY TEDDY BEAR-MAKING SUPPLIES" FROM BETH HAIKEN
http://www.ehow.com/eHow/eHow/0,1053,10429,00.html

BEARWORLD TIPS

http://www.bearworld.com/bearly_resource/index.html

You'll find advice on selecting fur, attaching eyes to your bear, and more at Bearworld.

TEDDY TUTOR FROM TEDDY BEAR DEN

http://www.teddybearsden.com/teddy-bears-den__teddytutor.htm

This site has tips and hints for beginners, plus a guide to bear-making terminology and a free bean bag teddy pattern.

TEDDY BEAR TIPS FROM THE PROS
http://www.bearartists.com/howto.html

Members of Bear Artists Online share tips on topics including dyeing mohair with Kool-Air, using glass beads and pellets, fashioning noses, sewing bears, and making patterns.

DO IT YOURSELF FROM TEDDY BEAR U.K.
http://www.teddy-bear-uk.com/lerfram3.htm

Learn to position a bear's eyes, nose, and mouth, as well as how to clean old mohair bears, protect your bears with an herbal moth repellant, and string joint miniature bears, at this great Web site.

BEAR FACTS—CHOOSING FUR FOR YOUR TEDDY BEAR BY JULIE WEGELIN
http://getcreativeshow.com/Crafting_Sewing_Conference_Center/craft_sewing_seminars/bear_facts.htm

Julie explains how the quality of fur can be described by length and density and tells you all the things you should consider when buying fur.

free Help Finding Doll And Teddy Bear-Making Patterns And Supplies

Judy adores shopping for dolls and doll-making supplies on the Web. Doll-making supplies can be tough to find in local stores or mail-order catalogs, especially if you're particular. Fabrics in ethnic skin colors, high-end teddy bear fleeces and furs, and the specialized fabric paints that doll artists use can be especially hard to track down—but not on the Web.

The best way to find a supplier for that obscure fabric paint or purple doll wig is to join one of the mailing lists in Chapter 4 and ask other doll-makers for recommendations. Many doll discussion groups maintain preferred mail-order and Web suppliers lists, and we've listed some in this chapter.

We've also included our own small list of Web stores that sell doll-making supplies. But please keep in mind that there are hundreds of retailers on the Web who sell doll-making supplies. We couldn't list them all, but could only provide a small sample to get you started shopping.

Web Auction Sites Are Dynamite Places to Shop for Doll Stuff

On any given evening you'll probably find Judy searching **eBay** (**http://www.ebay.com**) for French bed dolls from the 1920s, as well as their patterns and clothing. You can find anything in eBay and other Web flea markets. If you're a doll maker, you'll find patterns galore for dolls and doll clothes, especially vintage ones—everything from Barbie patterns to Holly Hobby patterns to clothing patterns for Betsy Wetsy. They're motherlodes of vintage doll patterns. You can find lots of good things to embellish dolls with too, such as vintage beads and plastic cameos (head to the "costume jewelry" category) or old linens and lace. You can also find vintage children's clothing, which can make ideal doll clothes, especially when embellished. To find all these things we suggest using the search feature on eBay's main page—the site is as large and jumbled as a giant fleamarket, with everything scattered every place. And check back every few days, since items up for auction change so frequently.

At the end of the chapter we've included a section with more tips for shopping for doll stuff on Web auction sites.

🧸 More of Judy & Gloria's Tips for Shopping for Doll Stuff on the Web

• If you're buying fabrics or patterns, try to stick to buying from a Web retailer who's affiliated with one of the major doll-making or collecting mailing lists, such as those we recommend in Chapters 3 and 4.

• When you shop on the Web, use a credit card if you can. That way, if you don't get your merchandise, you can complain to the credit card company and hopefully get a refund. Try to avoid paying with a check. Never pay with a money order.

• Look for the Better Business Online logo on Web shopping sites. That means that the Web site is a member of the BBB Online (**http://www.bbbonline.org**) and subscribes to their business practices. Most other "safe shopping" seals that you see on Web sites are little more than "fishing licenses"; the organizations that back them don't have the ability to follow-up on complaints or do background checks on the retailers they allow to use their logo. The BBB does.

• Read the eTrust privacy statement on retail Web sites, if the site subscribes to this program. The privacy statement will tell you what the Web retailer will do with any private information that you provide. In other words, the privacy statement tells you if the site plans to sell your e-mail address or physical address to other companies.

You can read more consumer tips about Internet shopping at these consumer protection Web sites:

THE BETTER BUSINESS BUREAU ONLINE
http:/www.bbb.org

THE FEDERAL TRADE COMMISSION
http://www.ftc.gov/ftc/consumer.htm
http://www.ftc.gov

INTERNET FRAUD COMPLAINT CENTER
http://www.ifccfbi.gov/

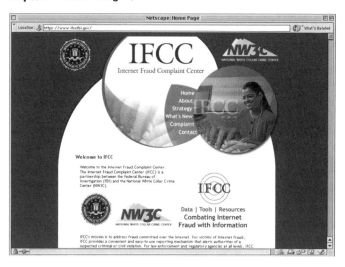

NEW YORK STATE ATTORNEY GENERAL'S INTERNET CONSUMER TIPS
http://www.oag.state.ny.us/consumer/consumer_issues.html

NATIONAL FRAUD INFORMATION CENTER (INTERNET FRAUD WATCH)
http://www.fraud.org

E-COMMERCE AND THE INTERNET
http://www.ftc.gov/bcp/menu-internet.htm

Ask Other Collectors on the Web for Shopping Recommendations A common topic on the doll mailing lists recommended in Chapter 4 is shopping recommendations for visitors to different cities. Don't be afraid to join the discussion and ask!

Directories of Retailers of Hard-to-Find Doll Making Supplies

THE DOLL MAKERS SUPPLIERS LIST
http://www.wtco.net/homepages/cocuzzo/suppliers.html

The Doll Makers discussion group offers a directory of members who sell supplies for doll crafters.

THE TEDDY BEAR TIMES' SUPPLIERS LIST
http://www.teddybeartimes.com

Click on "Suppliers" for a list of teddy bear parts mail-order suppliers in Britain.

THE CLOTH DOLL CONNECTION'S FABRIC AND SUPPLIES LIST
http://www.clothdollconnection.com/FabricandSupplies.html

Karen Samuelson offers links to doll body fabric and supply merchants around the Web.

FRIENDS OF DOLLNET'S GREAT STORES LIST
http://members.aol.com/tuckerdoll/stores.htm

Members of the mailing list Friends of Dollnet (you can read how to join them in Chapter 4) have compiled this directory of stores around the country that sell doll-making supplies. The list is organized by state. They include the addresses for the stores' Web sites. They also offer recommendations of Web-based stores.

BLUE MUSE CERAMICS
http://www.members.tripod.com/~Fibergal/index.html

Click the doll link for a large selection of porcelain doll making suppliers and supplies.

Just a Few of the Many Web Sites That Sell Hard-to-Find Doll-Making Supplies

🛒 JEAN & KEN NORDQUIST'S COLLECTIBLE DOLL CO.
http://www.jeannordquistdolls.com

The Collectible Doll sells supplies for porcelain doll makers, including paints, wigs, molds, eyes, and more.

🛒 CLOTHART
http://www.martydoll.com

You'll find fiber paints, pigments, embellishment fibers, and turning tools, as well as patterns for dolls by Tonya Boylan, Marty Donnellan, Susanna Oroyan, and Christine Shively, at ClothArt.

🛒 SPARE BEAR PARTS
http://www.SpareBear.com

This is where you can find hard-to-find teddy bear eyes and joints.

SEWSWEET DOLLS
http://www.caroleecreations.com

This is the home of Carolee and the patterns and kits for those adorable baby dolls with the soft-sculpted faces. If you've never made a Carolee doll, you've just got to try it. Their catalog offers a huge selection of hard-to-find doll-making tools and supplies, such as hair looms and eyes. The Web site offers a nice selection of links to other doll-making sites too.

 ## MINI WORLD DOLL SUPPLIES
http://www.miniworlddolls.com

You'll find a great selection of tools, supplies, wigs, eyes and lashes, clothes, shoes, and more. Be sure to check their wonderful selection of hints and tips. The site also includes a listing of upcoming doll shows and events.

 ## SISTERS & DAUGHTERS
http://www.sistersanddaughters.com

On this site, you'll find face-painting stencils, paints, "pieces and parts" (like fairy wings), and an online catalog of doll patterns from well-known (but sometimes hard-to-find) designers.

MONIQUE TRADING CORP.
http://www.monique.com

Monique sells eyes, shoes, wigs, and hosiery and other miniature accessories.

 BELL CERAMICS
http://www.bellceramics.com

Order hard-to-find porcelain molds and other doll-making accessories.

 NATURAL ARTCRAFT DOLL-MAKING SUPPLIES
http://www.nationalartcraft.com/dollmaking.asp

This site sells doll molds and other supplies.

Surf the Web Sites of Doll Artists for Great Patterns

© 2000 Kezi Matthews

*Many doll-makers, including Kezi Matthews (**http://www.thekeziworks.com**), sell patterns of their marvelous dolls at their Web sites.*

There are many, many, many doll artists who sell patterns from their Web sites. In most cases these aren't just the usual ragdoll patterns. On these sites, you'll find patterns for everything from wood nymphs to car mechanics, and a million exotic beauties in between. And chances are that you won't find them in any stores. We can't encourage you more: surf the sites of doll makers, look at the patterns they offer for sale, and try a few, even if they look difficult. You'll be surprised at what talent may be lurking hidden within your hands. The two best places to start your journey are:

KAREN SAMUELSON'S LIST OF CLOTH DOLL PATTERN MAKERS AT CLOTH DOLL CONNECTION
http://www.clothdollconnection.com/
ClothDollDesigners.html

Want a catalog from elinor peace bailey? How about "Annette the Lizard Lady"? Karen offers a clickable directory of dozens of doll artists, with particulars on getting catalogs and information from them. Some have Web sites, some do not.

DOLL NET
http://www.thedollnet.com

You'll find links to many doll makers' Web sites through the Doll Net directory.

▣ More Web Auction Sites for Doll Lovers

While **eBay** (**http://www.ebay.com**) is the biggest game in town, there are other Web auction sites worth checking out for dolls and accessories. On **Amazon.Com Auctions** (**http://auctions.amazon.com**) and on **Yahoo Auctions** (**http://auctions.yahoo.com**), you'll spot dolls up for sale. **Fairmarket** (**http://auctions.fairmarket.com**) is another auction worth checking.

There are several small Web auctions that cater to collectors of dolls and figures. One is **Mini Folks** (**http://www.minifolks.com**), where you'll find everything for Barbies to Beanies. **Theriaults.Com** (**http://www.theriaults.com**) specializes in auctions of dolls, teddies, and other toys. Auction catalogs, schedules, online auctions, and appraisal information are available.

Several Web services, such as **Auction Rover** (**http://www.auctionrover.com**), let you search and follow auctions on multiple auction sites. Search for "1965 Barbie", and AuctionRover will search a number of different Web auction sites looking for items. Other auction searches include **E-compare** (**http://www.ecompare.com/index-auction.html**) and **Bidder's Edge** (**http://www.biddersedge.com**). Tell **iTrack** (**http://www.itrack.com/**) to search auction sites for a particular item and the service will e-mail you when the item is up for bid. The disadvantage of these services is that they can be bedeviling to use. Also, some Web auction sites forbid these services' "robots" from searching their listings.

♨ Web Auction Sites Are Great Places to Bargain Hunt for Dolls and Doll-Making Stuff, But Before You Bid, Read Our Tips!

• **How safe is buying from Web fleamarkets?** It depends a lot on what you're buying, in our opinion. High-ticket items such as consumer electronics are high risk. Remember that in most instance you're not actually buying from the fleamarket, but from individuals who advertise on it. Your entire transaction will probably be with a stranger about whom you know nothing but an e-mail address.

• **Bid on auction Web sites that offer some kind of money-back guarantee.** A few of the auction sites offer compensation if you get fleeced. Ebay offers up to $200 on auctions in which the final bid is over $25. Amazon.Com's auctions (**http://auctions.amazon.com**) offer up to $250, but only on auctions that carry the Amazon Auction Guarantee logo—be sure to look for that logo before you bid!

• **Learn as much as you can about what you're buying.** Being knowledgeable about the sorts of things you bid on is your best defense against being sold something that's not what it's described as being. This is as true in cyber-fleamarkets as it is in in-person ones. Learn how to distinguish manufacturers' or craftsmans' marks. Learn the distinguishing qualities of the item you're collecting. Learn how to spot imposters.

• **Don't believe everything you read in descriptions.** One seller's "mint condition" may be your "shabby chic." One seller's "Victorian" hat box may be K-mart in disguise. While some fleamarket sellers tiptoe the line between poetic license and outright fraud, most are simply ignorant of what they're selling.

• **Ask what the item is made of, its dimensions, and how substantial it is.** Don't assume that the translucent bust of Napolean is crystal. Don't assume that the old-fashioned store sign is wooden. Don't even assume that the frying pan is iron.

Ask lots of questions about the item's size, weight, and composition before you bid.

• **If you doubt the authenticity of an item, ask the seller how they know it's so.** If an item is sold as a name-brand ceramic or porcelain, ask to see a scan of the maker's hallmark. If there are any identifying manufacturer's marks on the doll, ask to see a scan of them.

• **Never assume anything about an item's condition.** Something that looks great in a JPEG file on eBay may arrive in your mailbox demanding to be fumigated. Ask specifics about the item's state. If it's fabric, does it smell? If it's glass, are there any chips or hairline cracks? Do the doll clothes have any tears, moth holes, or worn spots? Does the doll have all its hair?

• **Be sure to ask too whether the item has ever been restored or repaired in any way.** That's something that dealers often neglect to mention in descriptions.

You can find some great stuff on Web fleamarkets like eBay—like these vintage red high-heeled bed doll shoes—but be sure to ask a lot of questions before you bid, especially in regards to shipping.

Tips on Selecting People to Buy From

- **Before you bid, check the seller's buyer ratings.** Web auction sites let buyers post comments about sellers after a transaction. Although these "buyer ratings" are often not what they're cracked up to be—they can be easily forged, and aggrieved buyers may be too timid to post negative feedback— if a seller boasts hundreds of happy customers, it can be a good sign that they will, in fact, send you your 99-cent buttons without laundering your check.

- **Avoid sellers who keep their feedback private.** Some services let sellers make bad feedback invisible.

- **Buy from sellers with a return policy**. Some sellers sell items "as is" and "no returns." Unless you can carefully check close-up photos, be wary.

- **Look at the seller's other auctions.** Some dealers sell only one type of collectible, like watches or toys. Sometimes you can get a sense from their other auctions whether they're experienced selling these types of items and whether their descriptions are accurate. Additionally, sometimes you can get a sense whether they're given to describing items with tacky come-on phrases and over-inflated claims.

- **Find out before you bid what the seller plans to charge for shipping and whether they will ship the item insured.** Amazingly, some sellers don't want to bother insuring items.

- **Avoid sellers who will accept only money orders.** If you send a money order you have no way of knowing that your money actually arrived in their hands and that they cashed the check.

- **Avoid sellers who will not agree to use an escrow service.** An escrow service acts as a middleman in the transaction.

You mail the check to the escrow service. The seller sends you the item. When you inform the service that you've received the item satisfactorily, the service forwards your check on to the seller. Some online auction sites offer this service for a modest fee. If you're buying a pricey item, you should ask the seller whether they'll use an escrow service before you bid. Two popular ones are iEscrow (**http://www.iescrow.com**) and TradeSafe (**http://www.tradesafe.com**).

• **Avoid sellers who use free e-mail services.** These include Yahoo, Hotmail, Excite, and Bigfoot.

• **Avoid sellers with bizarre e-mail handles.** If someone answers your e-mail with a weird e-mail name or an address like "Prince of Darkness," shop elsewhere. Listen to your gut. If you have any reservations at all about doing business with someone, don't bid.

• **Do not buy from anyone who e-mails you after you have lost an auction.** They may say, "I noticed you bid on such-and-such. I have some extra inventory. Would you like to buy it?" In these cases, they were using the auction as a come-on.

• **For high-ticket items, select sellers who will let you pay with a credit card.** There are advantages to paying by credit card. If you never receive the item, or if the item is defective, you can complain to the credit card company and get your money back.

• **Be skeptical of sellers who claim to be auctioning items off for a charity**. Charity scams abound on Web auction sites. A good tip-off of a scam is that the name of the charity isn't specified or sounds rather vague.

⚙ More Tips for Web Auction Bargain-Hunting

Check the "Ending Today" listings for the best buys. Most people bid on items in the last hours, or even the last minute, before an auction ends. (People who do their bidding in the last minute are called "snipers.")

Use the auction site's search engine if you're shopping for something specific. If you're looking for something particular, such as Holly Hobbie dolls and doll patterns (Judy collects those too), search the entire auction site for different words, combinations of words, shortened forms of words, and even misspellings. For instance, try "Holly Hobbie," "Hollie Hobby," "Holly doll," "Hobbie doll," and so forth. You should also try to think of all the offbeat ways someone might describe the peculiar sort of doll or accessory you're looking for, such as "bonnet doll."

Save all correspondence with the seller. Keep the URL of the Web page on which the item is posted, as well as its auction number. And keep in mind, before you bid, that if you get ripped off you'll have little if any recourse.

![bear icon] *What to Do If You Get Fleeced*

Where do you go if the "Victorian doll" looks like it came from Wal-Mart and the seller has stopped answering your e-mail? The first thing to do is to promptly report it to the Web auction site.

Ebay offers up to $200 compensation on auctions in which the final bid is over $25, but the service must receive a complaint within 30 days after the auction's close. Amazon.Com offers up to $250 compensation, but only on auctions that carry the Amazon Auction Guarantee logo.

Look for the Amazon Guarantee logo on auctions on **Amazon.Com**. *It doesn't guarantee that the item you're bidding on is authentic, but that you'll get your money back if you get taken—and the amount is under $250.*

Beyond this minimal insurance, the auction sites tend not to get involved in auctions that have gone awry, unless the seller is a repeat offender.

If the money involved is significant, there's a chance you might get law enforcement officials interested in helping you, but don't count on that either. Since Web auctions involve money mailed or transferred across state lines, contact postal officials, your local U.S. attorney's office, and the Federal Trade Commission. Be a pest, and call as many times as you need to get someone's attention.

That's why your best defense is to carefully choose what you bid on, and who you buy from.

How to Find An Out of Print or Otherwise Hard to Find Doll Pattern or Book on the Web

How can you find an out-of-print doll pattern or book on the Web? One of the first things to do if you know the name of its author, is to type the author's name into a search engine such as **Altavista** (**http://www.altavista.com**) to see if the author has a Web site. Another tactic is to join some of the doll-makers' mailing lists we recommend in Chapter 4 and post a message asking if anyone knows of the pattern's whereabouts. Here are more strategies for searching. We've had great success finding books and patterns through all these sites, so we recommend them whole-heartedly.

1. Try Hard-to-Find Needlework Books (http://www.needleworkbooks.com/)

Bette S. Feinstein has a huge collection of magazines and patterns going back to the 1900s, including *Needlewoman, Needle Arts—EGA, Needle & Thread, and Embroidery Magazine-UK*. Visit her Web site or e-mail hardtofind@needleworkbooks.com.

2. Try Bibliofind (http://bibliofind.com/)

You've probably heard people say you can find out-of-print books on **Amazon.Com** (**http://www.amazon.com**). But for out-of-print books, that site ain't nothing compared to this one. Bibliofind searches the catalogs of used book dealers around the country and within seconds comes up with hard-to-find titles. Prices tend to be reasonable, too.

3. Try Web Auction Sites Like eBay (http://www.ebay.com)

You'll find thousands of patterns, including old ones for knitting and crochet, as well as cross-stitch charts, books, and magazines lurking on Web auction sites like eBay. Use the main searcher to search for different words that may have been used to describe the pattern you're seeking. The trick is to check these sites nightly because items for sale change so fast.

4. Head to the About.Com (http://www.about.com) Special Interest Needlework Pages.

Meridel L. Abrams offers good-advice on how to search for out-of-print patterns on her cross-stitch pages (**http://crossstitch.about.com**). Click "Pattern Searchers" for her newest list of links.

Judy & Gloria's Tips for Fabric Shopping on the Web

Whether you buy doll fabric and teddy bear fur from retailers on the Web or through Web auction sites like eBay, buying it over the Internet has little relation to buying it in person. You can't touch it, you can't feel it. If it's a print, it can be hard to gauge the size of the print. If it's a fur, you won't be able to tell how soft it is. Here are some tips for Web fabric shopping:

• Some fabric stores do a better job of scanning fabric to post on their Web sites than others. Sometimes the fabric you get in the mail will look very different from what you saw on your computer screen. If you're buying fabric for a project where color and quality are critical, buy swatches first.

• If you see a fabric that you like on the Web site of a fabric manufacturer, print out the Web page and jot down all the details about the fabric, including the name of the company, name of the fabric or pattern line, phone number, and bolt number, and take it to your local fabric store. Some store owners may be willing to order it or track it down for you, although not all will do this. Many fabric makers post directories of stores that carry their fabric.

• If the fabric has a print, find out how large it is.

• If the fabric is second-hand, find out what condition it's in. Does it have any yellowing or fading? Any spots? How about signs of moths? Don't be afraid to ask what it smells like. Does it smell smoky or mildewy, or reek of mothballs? Antique dealers in cyberspace are used to "smell" questions.

• If it's a Web fleamarket find, once you get the fabric, clean it thoroughly (put it through the washer twice) and keep it from your other fabric in case it has moths.

 Web Sites of
Doll Magazines,
Clubs, and Museums

Can't find your favorite doll magazine at the newsstand? Tap into its Web site for articles, how-tos, and even live chats with other doll-lovers. Looking for a doll lovers' or makers' club in your community? Head to one of the many Web sites that offer directories of doll fanatics clubs around the world. You'll also find doll museums on the Web which serve up articles and photos about their collections.

 Web Sites of Clubs for Doll Makers

 INTERNATIONAL FOUNDATION OF DOLL MAKERS
http://www.ifdm.org/index.htm

Find out about membership, classes, and seminars at the Web home of this esteemed organization.

KAREN SAMUELSON'S LIST OF CLOTH DOLL CLUBS AROUND THE WORLD
http://www.clothdollconnection.com/ClothDollClubs.html

Find out about the Cheap & Easy Doll Club of Helena, Montana or the Ditzy Doll Tarts of Dallas at this cyber-directory of cloth doll clubs and their home pages around the Web. You'll even find links to doll clubs in Japan!

VICKY'S DOLL CLUB DIRECTORY
http://www.vicky-web.com/doll_club/main.html

Vicky in Florida maintains this list of doll clubs around the world. You'll find information on Internet-based doll clubs, as well as international ones and clubs in your own state.

THE ACADEMY OF AMERICAN DOLL ARTISTS
http://www.aadadoll.org/aadadoll/index.html

This group promotes original art dolls as an art form. Tap in to learn about workshops, membership, doll trade shows, and more.

NATIONAL INSTITUTE OF AMERICAN DOLL ARTISTS
http://www.niada.org

The NIADA promotes the art of the handmade doll. On the group's Web site, you'll find membership information, newsletter excerpts, and doll-making tips from members.

THE ORIGINAL DOLL ARTISTS COUNCIL OF AMERICA
http://www.odaca.org

The ODACA promotes doll artists and educates collectors about the art of doll making.

 ### INTERNATIONAL FOUNDATION OF DOLL MAKERS
http://www.ifdm.org

This organization for promoting the art of porcelain doll making publishes a magazine, and holds seminars, workshops, and other events.

MILLENNIUM DOLL ARTISTRY—INTERNATIONAL GUILD OF DOLL ARTISTS
http://www.dollartistry.com

This is a Web guild for artists who create dolls of color. There's an online gallery.

Web Sites of Clubs for Doll Collectors

UNITED FEDERATION OF DOLL CLUBS
http://www.ufdc.org

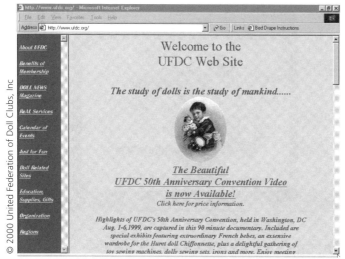

Tap into the Web site of this national organization for doll clubs to learn about doll collecting events and clubs in your area.

DOLL MAGAZINE'S GUIDE TO DOLL CLUBS IN THE UK
http://www.dollmagazine.com/clubs/index.htm

THE STEIFF CLUB, FOR COLLECTORS OF STEIFF BEARS
http://www.steiff-club.com

CAPERS N TEDDIES
http://www.capersnteddies.com/cntmain.html

Capers N Teddies is an international club for both teddy bear makers and collectors.

NATIONAL ANTIQUE DOLL DEALERS ASSOCIATION
http://www.nadda.org

JAPANESE AMERICAN DOLL ENTHUSIASTS
http://www.jadejapandolls.com

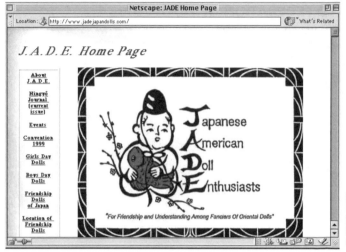

THE PAPER DOLL ARTISTS GUILD
http://www.opdag.com

There's advice for collectors, preservation tips, and a gallery of dolls.

MADAME ALEXANDER DOLL CLUB
http://www.madc.org

ORGANIZATIONS FOR MINIATURES ENTHUSIASTS
http://www2.dhminiatures.com/dhm/Clubs/Organizations.html

Dollhouse Miniatures maintains this guide to organizations for miniature lovers.

Looking for a Doll Club in Your Town?
The Bluebonnet Craft Network
(**http://bluebonnetvillage.com/dolls-1.htm**) offers an up-to-date and comprehensive list of clubs for doll makers around the country.

Web Sites of Magazines for Doll Makers

AUNTIE'S DOLLZINE
http://www.dollzine.com

An "e-zine" is a magazine you can read only on the Web, and Auntie's is a magazine for doll makers and lovers that you can read in entirely on its Web site. You'll read regular features on topics such as using the Barbie trademark on your Web site, how to promote your doll business on the Net, and discounting dolls.

DOLL MAGAZINE
http://www.dollmagazine.com

You'll find tips on doll-making, plus fun articles for collectors on the Web site of this leading magazine for doll makers and collectors. There's also a discussion board to talk to other doll lovers.

BEAR WORLD
http://www.bearworld.com

Read features and tap into free patterns from this print magazine.

THE TEDDY BEAR TIMES
http://www.teddybeartimes.com

Tap into the Web site of this British magazine for teddy bear makers and lovers for all sorts of wonderful features, from free teddy patterns to articles and an online discussion group for teddy fans.

DOLLS & MINIATURES MAGAZINE
http://members.aol.com/dollsinmin/index.html

Tap into the Web home for this magazine for doll and miniature makers and read tips on miniature making topics such as removing glue spots and using your husband's old wallet to fashion doll accessories.

DOLLMAKING
http://www.dollmakingartisan.com/dollmaking/index.htm

Dollmaking is written for the doll maker and costumer who enjoys creating contemporary, modern dolls. You can read articles from the current issue. There's also a discussion board.

TEDDY TODAY
http://www.teddytoday.com

Learn about this magazine for bear lovers and read articles from past issues.

DOLL ARTISAN
http://www.dollmakingartisan.com/artisan/index.htm

Doll Artisan is a magazine devoted to the reproduction of antique porcelain dolls. You can read articles from the current issue.

THE CLOTH DOLL MAGAZINE
http://www.theclothdoll.com/index.html

Logo © 2000 Internet Visions Company; site © 2000 The Cloth Doll Magazine

You'll find some great how-tos—like one on how to fashion life-like eyes—plus free patterns and an archive of past features that appeared in this wonderful magazine.

GILDEBRIEF
http://www.gildebrief.de/INDEX1.HTM

Gildebrief is a German magazine about antique reproduction doll-making techniques. It's published in English as well as German.

CUSTOM DOLLS ONLINE MAGAZINE
http://www.customdolls.net

This free online magazine offers lots of helpful how-to articles on topics such as how to make a display box for your doll. There are also interviews with doll makers.

THE DOLL PAGE DOLL ONLINE NEWS
http://www.dollpage.com/html/doll_news.htm

This Web magazine features news from many major doll companies.

MIMI'S LET'S TALK ABOUT DOLLMAKING ONLINE MAGAZINE
http://www.mimidolls.com/letstalk/letstalk.htm

Gloria J. "Mimi" Winer shares articles and book reviews in her online publication.

Web Sites of Magazines for Doll Collectors

DOLL READER MAGAZINE
http://www.dollreader.com

Read articles, get display tips, and find out about doll terms from this pre-eminent magazine for doll collectors.

DOLL NEWS MAGAZINE
http://www.ufdc.org

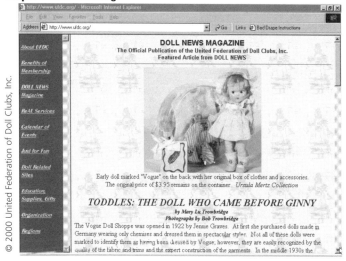

Tap into the Web site of the United Federation of Doll Clubs to read articles from the latest issue of its publication.

MILLER'S FASHION DOLL
http://www.millersfashiondoll.com

Read the latest news and gossip about your favorite fashion doll.

DOLL CASTLE NEWS
http://www.dollcastlenews.com

A bi-monthly magazine for doll and miniature collectors and those interested in doll making.

ANTIQUE DOLL COLLECTOR
http://www.tias.com/mags/adc

BARBIE® BAZAAR
http://www.barbiebazaar.com

Learn about this official magazine for Barbie® collectors and read feature stories.

FASHION DOLL SCENE
http://www.fashiondollscene.com

Learn about this print magazine for fashion doll collectors and read online features and articles for Gene, Madam Alexander, Candi, and other dolls. Fashion Doll Scene includes a listing of upcoming doll shows.

DOLLHOUSE MINIATURES
http://www2.dhminiatures.com/dhm

This print publication focuses on dolls and doll houses. At the Web site you'll find doll house tips, and a guide to the world of miniatures.

DOLL HOUSE WORLD
http://www.dollshouseworld.com

PAPER DOLL REVIEW
http://www.paperdollreview.com

ACTION FIGURE TIMES
http://www.primenet.com/~btn/aft.html

 Web Sites of Museums for Doll Lovers

🛒 THE DOLL MUSEUM IN NEWPORT, RHODE ISLAND
http://www.dollmuseum.com

All images and text on this site are property of The Doll Museum and may not be used without express permission.

Tap into the Web site of The Doll Museum to read articles about vintage dolls.

THE DELAWARE TOY AND MINIATURE MUSEUM
http://thomes.net/toys

Learn about this non-profit museum and view photos of some of its collection of miniatures, dollhouses, and toys dating from 1770 to 1960.

 🛒 **ROSALIE WHYEL MUSEUM OF DOLL ART**
http://www.dollart.com/dollart/index.htm

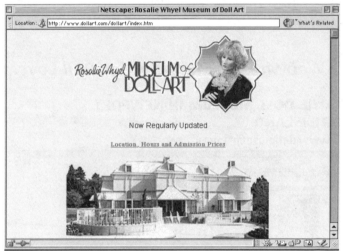

*Located in Bellevue, Washington, this museum showcases over 3,000 dolls, many on permanent display. The museum site (**http://www.dollart.com/dollart/control.htm**) offers a discussion board for doll fans and a gallery where you can view dolls from the museum's collection.*

SHANKAR'S INTERNATIONAL DOLLS MUSEUM
http://www.childrensbooktrust.com/dm.html

View pictures of some of the stunning dolls housed in this museum in New Delhi, India.

TOY AND MINIATURE MUSEUM OF KANSAS CITY
http://www.umkc.edu/tmm

AMERICAN MUSEUM OF MINIATURE ARTS
http://hometown.aol.com/minimuseum/museumhome.html

View the collection on the Web site of this museum, formerly known as the Doll House Museum of the Southwest.

PUPPENTOUR: THE BEST OF EUROPE'S DOLL AND TOY MUSEUMS
http://www.puppentour.com

Learn about this annual tour of the doll and toy museums of Germany and Austria.

free Patterns and Advice for Making Dolls and Bears for Charity

There's nothing more gratifying than stitching up a doll or teddy bear for a child who could use a bit of extra love. Numerous charities collect toys for fire departments, hospitals, and other caregivers to give to children in trauma. You can tap into their Web sites to learn how you can help. On the Web, you'll also find directories of charities in need of doll donations and free patterns for "emergency bears" that you can download and stitch. But don't forget to personalize them with a bit of yourself—a hand drawn face, a stitched message. Giving them to a child who needs them will be just like giving a bit of yourself.

Note: Many of the doll-makers who commune in mailing lists and discussion boards that we recommend in Chapter 4 organize regular charity projects.

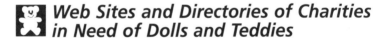 Web Sites and Directories of Charities in Need of Dolls and Teddies

TEDDY BEARS ON THE NET DONATION LIST
http://www.tbonnet.com/second_index.html

Teddy Bears on the NET maintains an up-to-date list of requests for teddy donations from hospitals, fire departments, and other charitable organizations in need of bears. Click the "Donating Bears" link on their home page.

BEARWORLD ADOPTED CHARITIES
http://www.bearworld.com

Bearworld, a Web e-zine for teddy lovers maintains a list of charities in need of teddies. Tap into their latest "issue" for the list.

GOOD BEARS OF THE WORLD
http://www.goodbearsoftheworld.org

Last year, Good Bears of the World gave away over 20,000 ted-dies to children who were victims of floods, tornadoes, hurricanes, and domestic violence.

TEDDYCARE INTERNATIONAL
http://www.teddycare.com

TeddyCare provides bears to police, fire departments and other community caregivers who come in contact with traumatized children.

TEDDY BEARS FOR CHILDREN
http://www.azgiftconnexion.com/tbears4children
http://www.onelist.com/group/tbears4children

"Nothing stops the power of a teddy bear" is the motto of this group, which collects teddies for charities. Tap into their Web site or their discussion group at OneList.

BEARS WHO CARE
http://www.alphalink.com.au/~suevill/bwc1.html

This Australian not-for-profit group gives bears to abused children.

SEWING WITH NANCY'S SEW A SMILE DIRECTORY
http://www.nancysnotions.com

Tap into the Web site of Nancy's Notions/Sewing With Nancy for an up-to-date directory of charities that could use hand-sewn items such as teddies and dolls.

INTERNATIONAL LEAGUE OF TEDDY BEAR COLLECTORS
http://www.iltbc.org

This non-profit organization is dedicated to providing teddies to abused and needy children and adults.

TEDDY CARE — YOUR COMMUNITY & YOUR CHILDREN
http://www.teddycare.com

Teddy Care also believes in spreading happiness through gifts of teddies to needy kids.

OPERATION TEDDY BEAR
http://www.angelfire.com/on2/OperationTeddyBear

Operation Teddy is always looking for donations of crocheted, knitted, or sewn teddies, dolls, and other toys for seriously ill children at Ronald McDonald Houses and hospitals. You'll also find a guide to free emergency teddy patterns available around the Web.

ALZHEIMER'S TEDDY BEAR
http://www.execulink.com/~remember/tedbear.htm

This London-based group gives teddies to people suffering from Alzheimer's.

TEDDIES MARCHING FOR A CURE
http://www.teddiesmarching.com

Learn about a teddy auction held each fall in Houston to benefit the Leukemia Society.

Learn about **Teddy E. Bear's Bold Journey for Breast Cancer Research**, *a unique project in which a teddy bear journeys across Canada to raise funds for cancer research (***http://www.teddyebear.org***). A poster of Teddy E. is available at the site, with proceeds going toward the cause.*

 Web Sites with Free Patterns for Teddies and Dolls to Give to Charities

HOME SEWING ASSOCIATION "EMERGENCY BEAR" PATTERN
http://www.sewing.org/careshare/stuffdolls.html
http://www.sewing.org/careshare/teddybear.html

The HSA offers a simple stuffed bear pattern for a toy that emergency medical technicians can keep on hand in an ambulance.

ANTONETTE CELY'S DOLLY HUGS PATTERN
http://www.cely.com/dollyhugs.html

ANTONETTE CELY'S BEAR HUGS PATTERN
http://www.cely.com/bearhugs.html

"Dolly hugs" is a salutation doll makers use at the end of e-mail messages, and it inspired doll artist Antonette Cely to design a special pattern for a doll to give children in crisis. Dolly Hugs' arms wrap around a child's neck and face, bestowing a little kiss. You can download the pattern for free from Antonette's Web site and give the finished product to a child that needs a hug. She has also designed a bear that hugs the child who holds him. The bear's arms wrap around the child's neck so that the bear's face presses against the child's cheek.

THE CARE WEAR PATTERN AND INFORMATION SITE
http://www.hood.edu/carewear

Learn how you can knit, crochet, or sew baby items to be given to needy infants, children, and their parents in hospitals. The site includes a directory of free patterns for you to make, including bunnies, bears, and more cuddlies.

TEDDIES FOR TRAGEDIES
http://www.fortunecity.com/millenium/lassie/322

This Canadian group is related to a project started by the Women's Royal Voluntary Services in England. Learn how you can donate knit or crocheted teddies to be given to suffering children around the world. You'll find free patterns for bears, as well as a message board, on the site. Be sure to take a look at the heart-warming pictures of bears distributed in Romania, Mexico, and Lebanon.

Visit More Web Sites Devoted to Charities.
Head to the **Earth Angel Charity Web Ring**
(**http://members.tripod.com/~countrycottagecrafts/
charityring.html**) to surf the Web sites of many more
charities.

free Patterns for Knitting and Crocheting Dolls, Teddies, and Their Clothes

Crocheted ball gowns for Barbie never go out of style. Neither do knitted sun dresses for American Girl dolls. And there is a charm to a knitted teddy bear that you won't find in fur. But the patterns to stitch up such confections can be so hard to find. But not on the Web! Knitters and crocheters have used the Internet to share such patterns since the dawn of cyberspace. You'll find patterns for bear sweaters and Teletubbies on many knitters' Web sites. Here are a few of our favorites.

KNITTING PATTERNS FOR TOYS AND DOLLS FROM ABOUT.COM
http://knitting.about.com/hobbies/knitting/library/bltoyspat.htm
http://knitting.about.com/hobbies/knitting/blknitlist.htm

The popular knitting mailing list discussion group KnitList has collected doll and teddy knitting patterns for years and shared them on the Net. Barbara Breiter of About.Com directs you to these patterns and shares a library of similar patterns donated by readers of About.Com. You'll find patterns for clothes for American Girls, Beanie Babies, Cabbage Patch Kids, Barbie, and teddies.

DOLL AND DOLL CLOTHES PATTERNS FROM WOOLWORKS
http://www.woolworks.org/dollpatt.html

Directions for knitting clothes for Barbies, plus a Beanie Baby sweater and more.

SASHA® DOLL ONLINE CLOTHES PATTERNS
http://world.std.com/~wam/sasha/index.html

Wendy McDougall shares knitting patterns for sweaters, a skirt, and socks, as well as patterns for go-go boots and shoes.

BABY DOLL JACKET AND BONNET
http://www.dollette.com/patterns/freebb.html

A free pattern for an adorable jacket and bonnet are available courtesy of Dollettes-n-Things.

JOYFUL KNITTED TOYS
http://members.xoom.com/jpleslye/knitting.html

You'll find a wonderful selection of patterns for knitted bears, Teletubbies, clowns, and other toys from Leslie of Australia.

KNITTING PATTERN FOR TELETUBBY PO
http://patriot.net/~annette/popattern/poprint.html

Complete directions for knitting your own Teletubby, also courtesy of Dollettes-n-Things.

18-INCH DOLL CLOTHES SET FROM NANCY HEARNE
http://www.nancyhearne.com/DrawingBoard/DClothes.htm

Nancy shares a photo and instructions for knitting a cardigan, a sweater, and pants.

TELETUBBIES KNITTING PATTERNS
http://members.xoom.com/jpleslye/tubbies.html

Leslie of Joyful Toys offers patterns you can use to knit your favorite Teletubby. Each stands 8 inches.

ANNE TUCKER BLAKE'S EDELWEISS AUSTRIAN JACKET FOR AN 18-INCH DOLL
http://www.knittingnow.com/edelpat.html

Your doll needs an Austrian jacket—yes, it does! Make it by tapping into this marvelous Web site for knitters.

DRESSING BARBIE® WITH GRANNIE
http://grannyshouse.net/dressing.htm

Patterns include a cape and hat made from worsted yarn, a hat and scarf, and knit dresses.

A KNIT SHAWL FOR 18-INCH DOLLS FROM MAGGIE'S RAGS
http://maggiesrags.com/freedollshawl.htm

Margaret K.K. Radcliffe shows you how to knit a lovely shawl for your doll.

BARBIE®'S WARDROBE FROM JUDY GIBSON
http://www.users.cts.com/crash/j/jgibson/knitting/barbie.htm

Get complete instructions (with photographs) for knitting hiking socks, a basic tube dress, a lacy party dress, and a rainbow ball gown.

JAN'S WOOL STUDIO
http://www.janeswool.com/pattern.htm

Jan offers an nice assortment of free doll clothes patterns, including knitted overalls and an evening dress for Barbie.

SUSAN'S KNITTING AROUND
http://mars.superlink.net/%7Esusana/Barbie1.html

Susan provides instructions for a basic raglan sweater, complete with a feather and fan section on the bottom, and matching pants.

FREE PATTERN FROM DOLL CROCHET PARLOUR
http://dollcrochet.rpmdp.com/free.html

Doll Crochet Parlour offers a large selection of patterns, including ones for a lacy dress, a parasol, a party dress, and a Cabbage Patch dress and booties.

PINEAPPLE AND SHELLS CROCHET DOLL DRESS FOR BARBIE® FROM ROSE V.
http://members.spree.com/tweetyrose/pineapplebarbie.html

FREE PATTERN FOR DOLL BALLERINA COSTUME
http://www.auntie.com/cnm/craftzine/ballerina.asp

This lovely two-piece outfit from Auntie-Dot-Com fits 18-inch dolls.

SUMMER PARTY DRESS AND SHAWL FROM JULIE A. BOLDUC
http://www.jpfun.com/patterns/13kids/doldres.shtml

Tap into these fashion doll crochet patterns from Julie.

PATTERN FOR FANCY CROCHETED DOLL STOCKINGS BY MARY LYTLE
http://home.flash.net/~liebling/stockings.htm

Crochet fancy stockings for 22- to 26-inch dolls. Perfect for historically costumed dolls.

Are Your Knitting or Crochet Skills Rusty?
If you're in need of a refresher course on knitting or crochet, or you'd like to learn these skills, visit **Illustrated Patchwork Crochet How-tos** (**http://www.patchworkcrochet.com/howtos.htm**). You'll find illustrated instructions that will get you hooking in no time. More illustrated crochet lessons for lefties as well as right-handers can be found on the Web site of **The Crochet Guild of America** (**http://www.crochet.org/lessons/lesson.html**). If knitting is a skill you wish to acquire, head to **Common Threads** of Encinitas, California (**http://www.fiberartshop.com/knclbg.htm**) for free knitting video lessons you can view on your computer. You'll need the RealPlayer browser plug-in from **Real Media** (**http://www.real.com**), but it's free.

free Help for Dollhouses

Pity the woman who grows up without memories of playing in a dollhouse. Gloria and her childhood gal-pal spent many hours playing in a dollhouse, baking magic cakes, sweeping the floor, talking to their Barbies, and in general preparing for adult life. Judy also played in a dollhouse—one built lovingly by her father. But unlike Gloria and her chum, Judy did not let friends into her dollhouse. No, no! It was her dollhouse, and she had no intention of sharing it. In her own way, Judy was preparing for adulthood too. Whether you build dollhouses for the child in your house or the one in your soul, there are Web sites out there to help flame the enchantment.

MINIATURES AT ABOUT.COM
http://miniatures.about.com/hobbies/miniatures

Subscribe to the Miniatures e-mail newsletter and read features on dollhouses and miniatures, all courtesy of Lisa Vollrath, About.Com's guide to miniatures.

🛒 "EVERYTHING YOU WANTED TO KNOW ABOUT DOLLHOUSES BUT DIDN'T KNOW WHO TO ASK" BY NANCY VAN HORN
http://www.miniatures.com/guide

Hobby Builders Supply (**http://www.miniatures.com**) *hosts this amazing site where you'll find a complete guide to finishing and outfitting your dollhouse, written by Nancy Van Horn. Nancy explains the different types of dollhouses, tells you how to paint, wire, and even wallpaper your dollhouse, and offers ideas and tutorials on installing flooring. She also offers dollhouse landscaping advice.*

MY MINIATURES
http://www.myminiatures.com

My Miniatures shows you the way to over 600 Web sites that offer dollhouse ideas and advice. You'll also find a directory of miniature clubs around the country, and information on their upcoming events.

DOLLHOUSE CENTRAL
http://www.worldramp.net/~wandy/dollcent.htm

Wanda Bell hosts a message board for dollhouse lovers and offers dollhouse tips and features.

REC.CRAFTS.DOLLHOUSES—THE WEB SITE
http://ares.redsword.com/dollhouse

Rec.Crafts.Dollhouses *is a popular Usenet newsgroup (head to Chapter 1 for directions on how to tap in). Dawn Duperault maintains FAQs, mail-order lists, and how-tos compiled from this discussion group through the years. This is a wonderful resource. You'll also find a directory of dollhouse associations.*

MINIATURES FROM SUITE 101
http://www.suite101.com/welcome.cfm/
dollhouses_and_miniatures

Bill Weiss hosts this site where you'll find feature articles, links, and a discussion area for dollhouse fans.

MINIATURE NET
http://www.miniature.net

There's a chat room for dollhouse lovers, as well as message boards and links to other Net resources, on this Canadian Web site. This site is also the home to the Miniature Net Web Ring, a linked collection of Web sites devoted to dollhouses.

JIM'S DOLLHOUSE PAGES
http://www.printmini.com

Searching for antique-looking maps, books, calendars, furniture, wallpaper, stained glass, office supplies, rugs, or quilts to accessorize your dollhouse? Head to Jim Collins' site. He offers a library of "printables"—miniature items you can print from within your browser, then assemble with paper and glue for your dollhouse. There's even a miniature pizza box you can make. Jim also shares a "photo journey" of his odyssey building an elaborate dollhouse. He shares his mistakes and tells you what he learned.

THE BUTTERCUPLETS HOME PAGE
http://www.miniature.net/buttercuplets/index.htm

Buttercup dollhouses are the focus of this site, but you'll find lots of advice on dollhouses in general. There's an archive of tips and a wonderful assortment of project instructions for making things like pictures, clothes, pillows, beds, and chairs for your house.

MINI SCENES AND THINGS
http://members.xoom.com/Boozrkitty/minithings.html

Suzanne Black offers project tutorials, tips, information about online classes, and a twice-weekly chat.

🛒 MOTT'S MINIATURES AND DOLLHOUSE SHOP
http://www.minishop.com

You can shop for all sorts of hard-to-find miniatures for your house, including furniture and electrical supplies, but you'll also find lots of good articles. Our favorites:

MAKING THE DOLLHOUSE DECISION
http://www.minishop.com/decide.htm

DOLLHOUSE WIRING TIPS
http://www.minishop.com/shop/Tiplight.htm

DOLLHOUSE ASSEMBLY TIPS
http://www.minishop.com/shop/tiphouse.htm

WHAT'S THE DIFFERENCE BETWEEN DOLLHOUSE BRANDS
http://www.minishop.com/Houses.htm

Head to the **Imagination Mall**
(**http://www.orchidmall.com/imagination**) for more
links to Web sites devoted to dollhouses.

SMALL STUFF MINIATURE DIGEST TIPS ARCHIVE
http://www.miniature.net/smallstuff/tips.htm

*Head to the search feature to find tips on dollhouse subjects, or
head directly to a category such as accessories, finishing, landscaping, or window treatments.*

MINIATURE PROJECT OF THE MONTH FROM THE
MINIATURE INDUSTRY ASSOCIATION OF AMERICA
http://www.miaa.com/how.htm

*You'll find all sorts of unique ideas for things to do with minia-
tures. Projects include "How to Make Oranges In a Bowl" and
"Creating Ponds and Waterfalls."*

Confused about what glue to use?
When assembling dollhouses and their furnishings,
glue is often a necessity. But which glue should you
use? **This To That** (**http://www.thistothat.com**)
offers gobs of glue advice. Select your project, click
a button, and the site will tell you about the appro-
priate glue. For instance, type in "fabric" and you'll
get three picks for glue, depending upon whether
you want your fabric to look crisp. There's also a
glue FAQ.

Web Sites of Organizations for Dollhouse and Miniature Lovers

 ## NATIONAL ASSOCIATION OF MINIATURE ENTHUSIASTS
http://www.miniatures.org

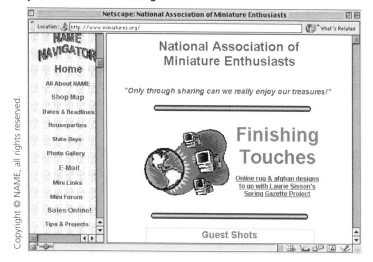

NAME is devoted to promoting the craft of miniature making. You'll find lots of tips on the site, as well as a bulletin board for miniature lovers.

COTTAGE INDUSTRY MINIATURE TRADE ASSOCIATION
http://www.igma.org

What's neat about this site is that, in addition to information about the association, you'll find a shopping guide, with a state-by-state listing of miniature retailers around the country.

MINIATURE INDUSTRY ASSOCIATION OF AMERICA
http://www.miaa.com/miaa

You'll find a retailer directory, monthly projects, and membership information.

INTERNATIONAL GUILD OF MINIATURE ARTISANS
http://www.igma.org

MINIATURE ENTHUSIASTS ACROSS CANADA
http://www.miniature.net/meac

 *Mailing List Discussion Groups for Dollhouse and Miniature Lovers*

Want to chat with other dollhouse lovers? Sign up for one of these mailing lists. The conversation will be delivered each day to your e-mail box, but first read our mailing list tips in Chapter 4.

TINY TALK MAILING LIST
http://www.tinytalk.org/tinytalk.html

SMALL STUFF MINIATURE DIGEST
http://www.miniature.net/smallstuff

DO IT YOURSELF DOLLHOUSE
http://www.people.cornell.edu/pages/erw4/DIY

MINIS FOR ALL
http://www.onelist.com/community/minis4all

MINI SHOP AND SWAP
http://www.onelist.com/community/MiniShopAndSwap

free Free Help for Sewing, Smocking, and Embellishing Doll Clothes

Maybe you've always wanted to stitch one of those exquisitely smocked doll gowns but were afraid of trying. Or maybe you couldn't find the proper supplies, such as the airy linen and the antique laces for inserts. In this chapter, we've assembled our favorite Web resources for stitching smocked and embellished doll gowns.

Your first stop should be **Delphi's Heirloom Sewing & Smocking Forum** (**http://www.delphi.com/heirloom/start**). You'll find other fans of heirloom sewing—the sewing of garments with fine linen and including such embellishments as smocking, pin tucks, lace insertions, and embroidery, done either by hand or machine. You'll also read articles, tutorials, and find patterns.

Quiltropolis (**http://www.quiltropolis.net/newmailinglists.asp**) runs several mailing lists for smockers and fans of heirloom sewing. Topics range from French hand sewing to lace shaping, sewing with silk ribbon and using pleaters.

Another good Web site to explore is Debbie Colgrove's **Sewing at About.Com** (**http://sewing.about.com**). Debbie offers how-tos and articles on smocking and heirloom sewing, as well as links to all the very best sewing resources on the Net.

*A good place to head for advice on smocking and other elements of heirloom sewing is the Sewing center at **About.Com**.*

Free Stuff for Hand Smockers

We've known a few hand-smockers and they all have this in common: they're earthy and pragmatic, but their very lives defy convention. No sewing machine smocked doll dresses for them! They take pride in the lovely garments they've so painstakingly hand stitched.

There are several cozy discussion groups for smockers on the Web. **WebSmockers** (**http://www.texoma.net/~reddish/**) has about fifty members. To join, one must be a member of the **Smocking Arts Guild of America** (**http://www.smocking.org/**). Dues are $10 a year.

You'll also find several smocking discussion groups on the big Web discussion service **eGroups** (**http://www.egroups.com**). To find them, click on "Arts & Humanities" then click on "Crafts." Scroll down the list to Smocking/Heirloom Sewing and the Smocking Newsletter and Digest.

THE SMOCKING CONNECTION
http://www.interlog.com/~gouldhop/smocking.html

You'll find beginner's smocking directions on choosing and preparing fabric, selecting thread, and gathering pleats.

CREATIVE SMOCKING ON THE INTERNET
http://www.smocking.com

This site is geared for retailers who carry smocking supplies—with information on the newest stuff and what's upcoming in smocking magazines. But if you can't find smocking supplies in your neighborhood, this site will lead you to retailers.

 ***Looking for Hard-to-Find Laces, Ribbons, and Other Supplies?*** There are many Web sites that sell some of the more esoteric heirloom stitching supplies, such as English and Swiss laces, ribbons for use in recreations of Edwardian millinery, and fluttery, fine linens. Some of our favorite sites: Victoria Louise, Mercers (**http://www.fred.net/stull/victoria.html**) and Garden Faries Heirloom and Special Fabrics (**http://members.aol.com/garfairies/heir.html**).

 If you're just getting started doing heirloom sewing, either by machine or by hand, tap into Lydia's Heirloom Sewing Center (**http://www.lydias.com/qheirbasics.html**) to read a glossary of heirloom stitching terms, plus advice on fabric, stabilizers, and thread.

Free Stuff for Machine Smockers

"SMOCKING ON THE SEWING MACHINE" FROM ELNA
http://www.elnausa.com/projects/98dec/dec98.htm

"HEIRLOOM HANDKERCHIEF AND BONNET" FROM ELNA
http://www.elnausa.com/projects/98aug/aug98.htm

 # *Free Help for Embellishing Doll Clothes*

Tap into these Web sites for advice and inspiration on adding ribbons, beads, and specialty stitches to your doll dresses.

NORDIC NEEDLE
http://www.nordicneedle.com

*In addition to being one of the world's best mail-order sources for hard-to-find specialty hand-stitching supplies, Nordic Needle offers hardanger tutorials on its Web site. You'll also find free hardanger stitching patterns online. You'll need the free Adobe Acrobat Reader (**http://www.adobe.com**) to view them.*

THE CHARTED DESIGNERS OF AMERICA GUIDE TO RIBBON EMBROIDERY STITCHES
http://www.stitching.com/CDA/Ribbon.htm

Ribbon embroidery can really spruce up a doll dress. It's a perfect way to stitch over tears in old linen and spruce up the dress at the same time. Tap into this Web guide for instructions on making those delicate buds and leaves.

🛒 DYED & GONE TO HEAVEN BY CARON
http://caron-net.com

Threadmaker Caron hosts a wonderful Web site filled with "online classes" that explore different embellishment techniques with Caron threads. Caron publishes an electronic magazine devoted to hand-stitching with colorful threads and ribbons. In the "how-to" section of the site you'll learn new stitches and techniques.

BEADNET
http://www.mcs.net/~simone/beadnet.html

Simone's BeadNet will link you into the marvelous world of beads and beading on the Net. There's also a guide to polymer clay-related Web sites.

KATHLEEN DYER'S COUNTED CROSS-STITCH, NEEDLEWORK & STITCHERY PAGE
http://www.dnai.com/~kdyer

This is one of the very best Web sites devoted to hand-stitching of all types. You'll find everything from how-tos to frequently asked question guides to hand stitching.

More of Our Favorite General Sewing Web Sites

You can find advice on just about anything on these sewing Web sites. You'll find other doll-makers to chat with, plus patterns, tips and links to other Internet resources on whatever your heart desires.

Head to Delphi's Sewing Forum for links to heirloom sewing information around the Web, as well as doll clothes sewing advice.

DELPHI'S NEEDLE & THREAD FORUM
http://www0.delphi.com/needle

Judy Smith's forum offers an active message board and chat feature for sewers, a directory of Internet resources for sewers, and much more.

SANDRA BETZINA ONLINE
http://www.sandrabetzina.com

Read columns and tips from sewing guru Sandra Betzina. You'll find lots of good stuff on her site, including a bulletin board for sewers and links to other Web resources for sewers.

 **NANCY'S NOTIONS ONLINE**
http://www.nancysnotions.com

Click the Sewing Room icon to read free articles or download free project sheets. There's also a very active message board for sewers.

Warning! **Beware of E-mail Offers to Make Money by Assembling Crafts at Home** *"Would you like to assemble crafts at home and get paid? Be your own boss! Top pay! Earn hundreds of dollars weekly! You can choose from—Beaded Accessories—up to $350.00 Weekly!—Holiday Crafts—up to $270.00 Weekly!—Hair Accessories—up to $320.00 Weekly!"* It's one of the most rampant Internet scams. You get an e-mail message promising you hundreds of dollars a week for assembling simple craft items. The catch? You need to buy a craft kit, usually for a hundred dollars or more. Once you assemble the items the company tells you your work is unsatisfactory—but you can keep assembling and sending them more items if you wish. Needless to say, your work is never satisfactory. And the craft items that you're supposed to assemble are so time-intensive, such as beaded hair bands, that no one could ever make a living making and selling them.

INDEX

.GIF 19
.JPEG 19
Advice
  auctions, 124
  cloth dolls, 66
  doll artists, 120
  doll care, 89
  e-mail scams, 171
  embellishing clothes, 168
  hard-to-find supplies, 119
  porcelain dolls, 80
  shopping online, 115
  out-of-print books, 130
AOL
  getting started, 7
  graphics tips, 12
  using, 8
Auctions, 114
Bookmarks, 24
  organizing, 27
Browsers, 16
Browser crashes
  fixing, 21
Browsers for older
  computers 17
Bulletin boards
  collectors, 54
  makers, 61
Cable modems, 14
Charity
  doll patterns for, 149
  donating dolls to, 146
Classes online, 69
Clubs
  doll makers, 133
  doll collectors, 135
Collecting
  specific dolls, 50
  teddy bears, 97
Consumer protection, 116
Desktop shortcuts, 25
Discussion groups, 61
DNS, 21
E-mail
  free, 15
  sending, 34
E-mail lists, 56

E-mail list rules, 57
E-mail list terms, 58
Error messages, 21
History of dolls, 95
ICQ, 63
ISP, 14
Magazines
  collectors, 141
  makers, 137
Mailing list services, 62
Manufacturers
  teddy bear, 104
Museums, 143
Newsgroups, 34
  America Online, 38
  Internet Explorer, 37
  Netscape, 35
Online safety 40
Patterns
  cloth doll, 71
  doll clothes, 77
  teddy bear, 108
Pricing, ISP, 14
Printing web pages, 29
Restoration, 94
Satellite, Internet via, 15
Saving pictures, 29
Smocking, 166
Supplies, 117
Tip
  accessing Web pages, 29
  AOL chats, 65
  AOL connections, 13
  auction tracking, 123
  browser security, 16
  cancer research bear, 149
  charitable
    organizations, 151
    charity Web sites 151
  choosing an ISP, 14
  clothing embellishment, 79
  doll appraisa,l 93
  finding doll clubs ??
  finding files, 28
  finding Web sites, 19
  glue, 162
  heirloom sewing, 167
  historical costumes, 79
  knitting and
    crocheting, 156

lace and ribbon
  supplies, 167
limited-edition dolls, 49
online fabric shopping, 131
polymer clay, 83
porcelain doll supplies, 87
read newsgroups in
  browser, 41
sculpting help, 85
teddy bear
  identification, 105
teddy bear sites, 103
updating browsers, 16
Web safety, 40
Web site directory, 42
URL, 20
Web rings, 55

For more information on other fine books from C&T Publishing, write for a free catalog:

C&T Publishing, Inc., P.O. Box 1456, Lafayette, CA 94549

(800) 284-1114

http://www.ctpub.com   e-mail: ctinfo@ctpub.com

ABOUT THE AUTHORS

Judy Heim has been making dolls and teddy bears for over 20 years. She's the author or co-author of 14 computer books, including *The Needlecrafter's Computer Companion*. She's written for *PC World* magazine for 15 years, and for 10 years authored a monthly Internet column for the magazine. She has written for *Family Circle, CNN Interactive, Newsweek, Cosmopolitan, PC/Computing, Family PC,* and many other magazines.

Gloria Hansen is the co-author of 10 Internet or computer-related books, including *The Quilter's Computer Companion*. Gloria is also an award-winning quiltmaker. Her work—often designed using a Macintosh computer—has appeared in numerous magazines, books, and on television. She has written for leading computer magazines (including *Family Circle* and *PC World* and craft publications (including *Art/Quilt Magazine* and *McCalls's Quilting*, and she writes the "High-Tech Quilting" column for *The Professional Quilter*. You can visit her Web page at **http://www.gloriahansen.com**. Gloria lives in East Windsor Township, New Jersey.

BIBLIOGRAPHY

Heim, Judy and Gloria Hansen, *Free Stuff for Quilters*, C&T Publishing, Concord, CA,1998

._____. *Free Stuff for Crafty Kids* C&T Publishing, Concord, CA,1999

._____. *Free Stuff for Sewing Fanatics,* C&T Publishing, Concord, CA,1999

._____. *Free Stuff for Stitchers,* C&T Publishing, Concord, CA,1999

._____. *The Quilters Computer Companion,* No Starch Press, San Francisco, CA, 1998

Heim, Judy, *The Needlecrafter's Companion,* No Starch Press, San Francisco, CA, 1999

FREE STUFF ON THE INTERNET SERIES

Free Stuff for Sewing Fanatics

This volume of the Free Stuff on the Internet series is full of information on how to get great free stuff on all kinds of sewing topics, including tailoring and fitting, serging and sewing machine help, home décor sewing, dollmaking patterns and tutorials, fabric embellishment, sewing for kids and pets, and bridal, vintage, and heirloom sewing.

Free Stuff for Quilters, 2nd Edition

Learn how to get on the Internet and locate the quilting-related sites that offer the best free stuff! You'll includes over 150 updated and new links, along with information on topics such as quilt patterns and tips, discussion groups, guilds, organizations, quilt shops to visit when you travel, quilt and textile galleries, and how-tos for fabric dyeing, painting, stamping, and photo transferring!

Free Stuff for Stitchers

The second entry in our popular series will teach you how to get on the Internet and how to find the stitching sites with the best free stuff! It includes cross-stitch and embroidery, knitting and crochet, spinning, weaving, rug making, dyeing and painting, stenciling, stamping, dollmaking, beading, lacemaking, and tatting.

FREE STUFF ON THE INTERNET SERIES

Free Stuff for Crafty Kids
The Free Stuff on the Internet series by Judy Heim and Gloria Hansen helps make it easy to stay organized as you visit sites that offer free patterns, articles, E-mail, advice, galleries, and more! This volume is your complete Internet guide to kid-friendly crafts, such as coloring books and scrapbooks, paper airplanes and kites, making paper dolls–and accessories, puppet making, juggling and magic crafts, origami, cartooning, and balloonart tutorials.

Free Stuff for Collectors
Includes Web sites just for collectors, such as discussion groups for collectors, collectibles market news and specialty magazines, determining the value of your collections, tips for cleaning and restoring, storing and insuring your collections, researching the authenticity and history of collectibles, and tips on how to find, buy, and sell collectibles.

www.ctpub.com

FREE STUFF ON THE INTERNET SERIES

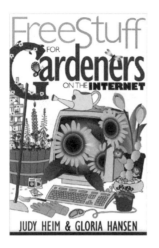 

Free Stuff for Gardeners

Web sites for everything gardening, including gardening tips and discussion groups, tips for orchid fanatics; special topics such as indoor, aquatic, and organic gardening; where to find rare plants; how to tackle the eccentricities of your growing zone; ideas for landscaping and caring for lawns, bushes, shrubs, and trees; and growing annuals, perennials, bulbs, roses, and vegetables.

Free Stuff for Home Decor

Great sites that focus on home décor and improvement, including everything for walls, windows, floors, and furniture; projects, tips, advice, and discussion groups; web sites associated with TV shows, radio programs, and magazines; special interests like home storage, feng shui, decorating for the holidays, and more!

www.ctpub.com